Property of Fran Donovan
bought from
Daughters of St Paul
9-6-78

65 Carol Dr.
Dedham Mass 02026

THE CHURCH–LIGHT OF ALL MANKIND

THE CHURCH

Light of All Mankind

POPE PAUL VI

Compiled by the
Daughters of St. Paul

ST. PAUL EDITIONS

Texts of the Pope's speeches
N. C. W. C. Translation

Library of Congress Catalogue Card Number: 67-29691

Printed in U.S.A. by the *Daughters of St. Paul*
50 St. Paul's Ave., Jamaica Plain, Boston, Mass. 02130

172 Tremont St., *Boston, Mass.* 02111 - 381 Dorchester St., *So. Boston, Mass.* 02127 - 325 Main St., *Fitchburg, Mass.* 01420 - 78 Fort Place, *Staten Island, N.Y.* 10301 - 625 East 187th St., *Bronx, N.Y.* 10458 - 39 Erie St., *Buffalo,* N.Y. 14202 - 202 Fairfield Ave., *Bridgeport, Conn.* 06603 - 141 West Rayen Ave., *Youngstown, Ohio* 44503 - 415 Euclid Ave., *Cleveland, Ohio* 44114 - 2700 Biscayne Blvd., *Miami, Florida* 33137 - 86 Bolton Ave., *Alexandria, La.* 71301 - 114 East Main Plaza, *San Antonio, Texas* 78205 - 1570 Fifth Ave., *San Diego, Calif.* 92101 - 278-17th St., *Oakland, Calif.* 94612
1063 St. Clair Ave. West, *Toronto, Canada*

CONTENTS

PART I

POPE PAUL ON THE CHURCH

Part II

INTRODUCTION

What is the Church?

Who are the People of God?

What is the Church's attitude toward the modern world?

How does the Church contribute to progress and the advance of social justice?

As a father and guide Pope Paul VI answers these and many other vital questions. His inspiring words show how the Church "reflects the Light of Christ all over the world," and how those who seek to know the Church "with a loving eye for the truth, cannot but acknowledge that she carries in herself a message of universal and single light, one liberating, necessary and divine."

This timely book is drawn from talks given by Pope Paul at his general audiences. The Pope's wise and revealing statements provide authoritative answers and guidelines for everyone—clergy and laity—in this post-conciliar age of change and renewal. The final pages of this valuable book contain the thought and message of Vatican II about the Church.

Pope Paul on the Church

THE HERITAGE OF VATICAN II

BELOVED SONS AND DAUGHTERS, in these reflections, which the weekly general audience gives us an opportunity and stimulus to make on the recently ended Second Vatican Council, we ask ourselves what were the most evident marks of its spirit. In other words what were the inspiring principles which promoted, permeated and guided it so as to impress on it a doctrinal and moral aspect which distinguishes it and defines it and will cause it to be remembered in history.

The present week, dedicated to the union of all Christians in the one Church founded by Christ, suggests to us that the ecumenical spirit was one of the principal characteristics of the council. This is so not only because it was called ecumenical in canonical terminology, because it was so designated as a convocation and gathering of the Catholic bishops of the entire world, but also because the council was motivated by the intention of smoothing the way for reunification in the one flock of Christ of the very many Christians who are still separated among themselves as well as from our communion.

This intention is now called ecumenical, as is that of the various ecumenical movements which, especially in our century and outside the Catholic Church, aim at the reconciliation of the various Christian confessions which are divided among themselves.

In this connection we should remember the hope which gave Pope John XXIII of venerated memory the courage to convene the ecumenical council. He wrote in his encyclical, *Aeterna Sapientia*: "It is precisely for the purpose of making the Church more suitable for accomplishing in our times its lofty mission (of seeing all peoples onto the path of truth, charity and peace) that we have resolved to convene the Second Vatican Ecumenical Council, trusting that the solemn gathering of the Catholic hierarchy will not only strengthen the bonds of unity in faith, worship and government which are the prerogatives of the true Church, but will also attract the attention of innumerable believers in Christ and invite them to gather around 'the great Shepherd of the flock' (Heb. 13:20) whose perennial custody has been entrusted to Peter" (AAS 1961, p. 799).

We may well say that this ecumenical spirit—which tends to expand the heart of the Catholic Church beyond the framework of its actual hierarchical communion so as to give it the universal dimensions of the design of God and the charity of Christ—has permeated the council. This potential ecumenicity has enveloped and inspired the concrete ecumenicity of the Church gathered in council.

An anxiety for universality has inspired its stupendous words concerning the People of God, kindled in its heart a missionary fire which radiates from every conciliar document and prompted it not only to accents of humility, forgiveness, understanding and a search for all Christians, but also to words full of respect and love for all followers of non-Christian religions (cf. Cardinal Marella: "The Role of the Council in the Future of Non-Christian Peoples").

Indeed, this spirit has prompted it also to utter words for the world; yes, for the secular world as it exists today, for which the Church had messages designed to overcome any distance, to surmount any obstacle: "Their voice has gone forth unto all the earth" (Rom. 10:18).

Two conciliar events demonstrate most clearly the ecumenical spirit of the great synod. The first was the presence in the conciliar assemblies of many observers, the representatives of various separated churches and of the various Christian communities, a presence which had not been seen for centuries, an exemplary and moving presence which stimulated in the council Fathers attitudes of re-evaluation, esteem and affection such as have not been expressed for a long time. It was a presence which seemed to us to be filling the spirits of those attending with eagerness, a sense of commitment and hope—the ecumenical spirit.

The other event was the *Decree on Ecumenism,* a document which clarifies doctrine on this most important theme, expounds the principles of Catholic ecumenism, indicates ways for exercising it worthily and outlines the relations existing between the Catholic Church and the separated brethren, laying the basis for a new, sincere and cordial dialogue with them.

These things we all know by now. But all of us must reconsider them. They are not things of the past, nor do they concern others. They are our own things, which concern not only the shepherds of the Church but also the faithful.

They impose on us, even prior to an approach to the separated brethren, a personal and collective renewal of Christian life. This *Decree on Ecumenism* says: "In ecumenical work Catholics must assuredly be concerned for their separated brethren, praying for them, keeping them informed about the Church, making the first approaches toward them. But their primary duty is to make a careful and honest appraisal of whatever needs to be renewed and done in the Catholic household itself in order that its life may bear witness more clearly and faithfully to the teachings and institutions which have been handed down from Christ to the Apostles" (n. 4).

We should now like to ask you to meditate on the attitude to be observed regarding this ecumenism, of which there is now so much talk and on which the unity week gives us an abundance of information and exhortations.

There are several possible attitudes. There is one of indifference and lack of interest, often due to scant knowledge of the questions and of their complexity. In this respect, we would simply say: It is necessary to know. It is necessary to instruct oneself. It is no longer permissible to ignore a question of such importance and topicality.

On the one hand, there is an attitude demonstrating an excess of enthusiasm and over-simplification, as if contact with the separated brethren were easy and without danger, as if the immediate establishment of concord and collaboration would result from ceasing to attach importance to doctrinal and disciplinary matters. This attitude is wrong because it can bring about illusions and delusions, weaknesses and a conformism not at all beneficial to the cause of true ecumenism.

There is also the attitude of the diffident and the skeptical. Some fear that ecumenism may entail criticism and revision of the truths of the faith, disregard for Christian traditions and teachings, and conformism to the religious concepts of others at the expense of one's own. Still others fear it is vain to hope for the effective re-establishment of one sole religious belief and a unique and true ecclesial communion. Too many things divide us from the separated brethren, they say. Too much time has passed since the breach—by now unbridgeable—and one should not expect the miracles which would be needed for true reconciliation.

This attitude is prompted by serious considerations, but it is wrong too because it is not in accordance with the spirit of the times or the needs of our day. Above all, it is not in accordance with the will of Christ. The council is solemn on this point!

The right attitude, then, is to follow the directive line which, in practice, the Church proposes to us and prescribes for us with good norms. But this trust in the guidance of the Church in ecumenical matters presupposes and demands a psychological disposition which, though complex and difficult perhaps, we will sum up in one well-known and quite sacred word: love.

To bring about ecumenical progress within the bounds of the integrity of doctrine it is indeed necessary to love. It is with this resolution of love in Christ that we today send our greetings to all the separated brethren and that we bless you wholeheartedly, beloved sons and daughters.

THE PEOPLE OF GOD

BELOVED SONS AND DAUGHTERS, every meeting of a religious nature—but especially this weekly meeting which makes us consider the number and kind of its participants—reminds us of the concept which the ecumenical council wanted once again to teach widely and almost to proclaim in reference to the "people of God."

Here, we say to ourselves in viewing all of you present, here is a part of God's people!

You know how modern culture has studied and praised this concept of the "people" in its various aspects: ethnical, social, national, political, etc.

You also know how in the religious field the idea of the "people" saw great development and had various interpretations.

What interests us is the idea which God Himself deigned to reveal to us historically by putting His plan of salvation into effect first in the Old Testament and afterwards in the New Testament.

God does not save mankind outside of a collective plan, but within a plan in which each single soul is part of a community chosen and aided by God.

The council says: "God wished to sanctify and save mankind not individually, not without any bond between one another, but wished to constitute men together as one people who would acknowledge Him in truth and serve Him faithfully. Thus He chose for Himself the people of Israel" (Constitution on the Church, n. 9).

Christ, as we know, instituted a new covenant between God and mankind, calling to make up the people of God persons of all nations, not linked by bonds of race or blood but by a single faith in the word of God, by a single Spirit and by a single social body, called the Church, as the "visible and imprescindible sign of unity" (S. Cyprian, Ep. 69, 6; P. L. 3, 1142).

Now, this new people, to whom all of us are fortunate to belong, is a people of "saints," of "the consecrated," of "living stones," who form the "spiritual house" of God, of souls clothed with a holy priesthood that befits them to offer spiritual sacrifices pleasing to God through Jesus Christ (cf. 1 Pet. 2:50).

It is the "royal priesthood" (ibid. 9) which is so much spoken of today and rightly recognized as the prerogative and representation of the sacred and incomparable dignity of every Christian in reference to any other earthly dignity.

That the words now referred to are found in the first papal encyclical, that is to say, in the first letter of the Apostle Peter to the Christians of Asia; and that St. Ambrose, among others, states that "all children of the Church are priests" (Exp. in Lucam, V, 33), thus able to deal with God and offer themselves to Him as a sacrificial gift (cf. Rom. 12:1), is not a new thing.

We would do well to read and meditate on the beautiful pages of the council's *Constitution on the Church,* devoted to the people of God, from which emerges not only the excellence of the people themselves, but also that of each individual soul, of each individual life therein inscribed. The wonderful title of "faithful" distinguishes and lends extraordinary spiritual beauty to the Christian who endeavors to be conscious of his vocation and wishes to be consistent with it: faithful.

This is the name—greatly emphasized by the council—that brightly shines before our spiritual glance when, as at this moment, we find ourselves surrounded by citizens of God's people. This is a name that fills us with wonder, with reverence, esteem, affection, faith and joy.

Here is the Church, we tell ourselves. Here is the assembly of the faithful, in other words, of those called to God's kingdom, of those elected as the adoptive children of God and elected to the profound and sweet brotherhood of the charity of the Lord.

Here are the souls kindled by the inner flame of the Holy Spirit. Here are those marked by the character of Christians, by that of witnesses of the new life, by that of persons destined, if they so wish, to the divine and eternal life.

Here is the "personality conferred upon the Christians. Here is the basis of his rights and duties." Here are the faithful, here are the people of God!

Beloved children, why do we say these things to you? We say them so that you will know how welcome your visit is to us and what a consoling and edifying effect it produces in our heart. You come as the faithful. Thank you, thank you, O Faithful of Christ and of Holy Church!

We say these things to you so that you may read and study them in the great pages of the council texts and because it seems to us that we could not say anything better to you. We revive in you a perhaps slumbering consciousness of what you are. We call you back to the sense of your Christian dignity, to the pure and sacred character of your persons, to the duty of preserving at all times, under any conditions of secular life, the pledge of the name that defines you: the faithful. And faithful may you be, beloved children, to the honor and status that Christ has accorded to you and which the Church recognizes in you and upholds.

And as the faithful, beloved children, we bless you.

THE HOUR OF THE LAITY

BELOVED SONS AND DAUGHTERS, just as Our Lady pondered in her heart—"But Mary kept in mind all these things, pondering them in her heart" (Luke 2:19)—the events that had surrounded the birth of the Savior, so we, with the humble intention of imitating to some extent that learned and incomparable innermost consciousness, are thinking over the teachings of the council, an event very provident and great for the rebirth of Christianity in our times.

Notable among the things which we deem worthy of being remembered and understood by everyone are, in our opinion, those that refer to the laity, in other words to the faithful who have not received sacred orders, nor connected themselves with the religious state.

They are the greater part of the people of God. They are the Christians who live in the world, they are the "laymen" who are chiefly interested in temporal matters and who are engaged in activities not exactly sacred, but secular.

The council, as you know, devoted great attention to the laity, in such manner and measure as to be noted as an innovation in the life of the Church.

It is not that the council said things that were new and previously unknown. The innovation in this respect, consists in the fact of expressly having dealt with the laity, and to have made evident the marvelous doctrines which, in God's Church, refer to the laity: their natural and supernatural dignity; their sacred nature, in fact, their "priesthood"; in other words, their ability to exercise a spiritual cult by professing the faith, by offering to God prayers worthy of being heard, by bringing to full development the fruits of charity, etc.

In other words, their Christian "personality," with its many rights and duties, has been put in a splendid light which it will be well to know and admire.

We have spoken of this at other times and, God willing, we will speak of it again. We have particularly recalled how the single fact that a human being is a Christian gives rise to a vocation toward Christian perfection, toward sanctity for him. But this is not all.

A trait of the council in reference to the laity, which we might almost call original because it stresses it so greatly, is that it calls for another vocation for the laity: that of the apostolate.

It is something which appears strange and not very agreeable to some because it attributes to the laity too many duties and too many obligations. Yet the council precisely devoted no less than one entire decree to the apostolate of the laity.

This not only for the usual historical or contingent reasons deriving from the necessity of promoting the cause of religion in the modern world—which is so easily and largely drawn from it—but rather from intrinsic reasons, in other words, because of the very fact that one is Christian.

From the Christian character itself there ensues the duty and right of exercising an apostolate. The apostolate almost becomes identified with the vitality which is proper of a Christian.

Formerly, Pius XI, in developing the concept of Catholic Action, had mentioned this requirement, almost equating Christian life and apostolic action.

The council is very explicit not only in the *Constitution on the Church* (ch. 4) but also in the decree mentioned above, where we read: "The Christian vocation . . . is by its very nature also a vocation to the apostolate" (n. 2).

Furthermore: "The laity derive their rights and duties with respect to the apostolate from their union with Christ their Head."

In fact, "having been incorporated into the Mystical Body of Christ through Baptism and strengthened by the power of the Holy Spirit through Confirmation, they are assigned to the apostolate by the Lord Himself. . . ."

"Therefore, on all Christians is laid the splendid burden of working, to make the divine message of salvation known and accepted by all men, throughout the world" (n. 3).

And further still: "But the laity, by their very vocation, seek the kingdom of God by engaging in temporal affairs and by ordering them according to the plan of God. They live in the world, that is, in each and in all of the secular professions and occupations.

They live in the ordinary circumstances of family and social life, from which the very web of their existence is woven. They are called there by God so that . . . they can work for the sanctification of the world from within, in the manner of leaven" (Constitution on the Church, n. 31).

What a subject for reflection for all! Truly such a doctrine can renew the life of the Church and, to a certain degree, change the face of the world from its dark and negative aspects.

Every Christian must become active and interested in the welfare of others, supporting the spiritual mission of the Church. Every conscience must be stirred by an inner sense of responsibility and heed the inner life of the Christian call, saying: It is up to me, it is also up to me to do something for God's kingdom.

The slothful mentality of a Christian who wants no worries, who does not want to be concerned with the good of others, who does not wish to be zealous, should disappear.

Self-centered spirituality, concern for public opinion, the attempt to minimize one's own duties toward the Church and the social apostolate should give way to an always vigilant desire for good, for courageous and continuous endeavor to dare to make some gesture which will be useful to others.

They should likewise give way to a humble and willing adherence to already organized forms for the apostolic action of the laity.

What a spiritual mobilization! What a transformation of the Catholic community! What a sum total of moral energies would thus be given to the modern world!

Let each one think of this. The forms of the apostolate are many and varied.

Let each ask himself: Which is the right one for me?

May our apostolic blessing obtain for you the light and strength to respond well to the vocation of the hour which has by now been sounded, the hour of the layman.

THE CHURCH'S ATTITUDE TOWARD THE MODERN WORLD

Beloved sons and daughters, since the council, as you know, the question of the relations between the Church and the world has become more immediate.

The great *Pastoral Constitution on the Church in the Modern World,* which was discussed and approved at the end of the council, indeed presents this question in its fullest terms, touching on a number of doctrinal, moral and practical problems, some of an ancient and perennial interest, others of a topical and contingent importance.

It is this very extensive and formidable discussion which has centered on the council not only the attention of the faithful but also that of the outside world. It also demonstrates to those who have no religion how alive the Catholic religion is in itself and how it adheres to the realities, spiritual and temporal, of human experience.

The science of man, philosophy, history, ethics, sociology, culture in general, the "earthly realities" as they are now called, are placed by the council under the beam of light of Catholic theology for a new and daring judgment, for an effort at understanding and analysis, for an act of study and discovery which the teaching authority of the Church had never before accomplished in so direct, systematic and authoritative a way. It will be a matter for reflection for everyone for many years to come.

In this brief moment we will restrict ourselves to pointing out how the simple fact of the question being raised gives rise to further mental questioning, now widespread among scholars and others, regarding the fundamental attitude of the Church toward the world. Is it an attitude of condemnation, of separation, of indifference, of acquiescence, of understanding, of alliance?

The reality which is called the "contemporary world" is too complex for a simple single answer. The Church is positive in her judgments. She does not prejudge. She is not superstitious or superficial. The Church knows that in the world, that is to say is our human reality, there are many faults and many evils. She does not ignore all the arguments for modern pessimism. Indeed she rather reveals their fatal and radical cause—original sin.

She teaches, in accord with all the most sincere and implacable diagnoses of the human intellect and earthly history, that the evils of man are profound, recurrent and themselves incurable. The Church knows the abysses of sorrow, sin and death. She can see the depths of human injustices, of personal and social miseries. She knows how to denounce fearful threats from the "powers of darkness." She knows how to call things by their proper name—often painful, ignoble, criminal. She knows how to cry. The liturgy can have moving and tremendous things to say to us in this respect.

Indeed the Church does not deny a pedagogy and an asceticism of her own of "contempt for the world," which played such a great part in medieval education for the liberation of man from the materialism and animalism of pagan and barbarian life. The Church will continue to note the spiritual detachment which must intervene between the Christian orientated toward "the kingdom of heaven"—that is to say, toward the life of the spirit and the eschatological life beyond time —and the self-sufficient concept of earthly life, that is to say, a world satisfied with itself and entirely bent on the transient and deceitful goods of this earth.

That is why it has become customary to speak of the "Church of the poor" as the ideal Church, as well as to attribute to the "Constantinian Church" reprovable temporal contaminations (although the expression is quite unsuitable and seems to disregard the great historical fact of the initial liberty of the Church).

All this is true and remains. But we cannot forget the optimism—we should say the love—with which the world of the council looks to the world in which it finds itself and which surrounds it, overwhelms it and oppresses it with gigantic and overpowering phenomena.

This is one of the salient aspects of the council. It considers the world in all its realities with a loving attention capable of discovering everywhere traces of God and therefore of goodness, beauty and truth. This is not only its philosophy, it is its theology. Behold this is what Revelation is for! The light of the Gospel illumines the panorama of the world. The shadows are there, terrible and strong, sin and death above all. But everywhere that that light rests, there is the reflection of God. The Church seeks it, grasps it and delights in it.

The Church finds this reflection in the cosmos as well. Nobody can be attracted by the fascination of the universe like a true Christian can. There his glance meets the flashing glance of God the Creator, who according to the Scriptures, "saw all the things that He had made and they were very good" (Gen. 1:31).

The Church's glance turns to the face of man and there especially perceives the divine reflection. She turns to the history of mankind and there finds a chain of events through which there runs an impulse leading to Christ and centering in Him.

She turns indeed on the modern world without fear and without recoiling, contemplating, rather, and blessing. She considers and blesses the work of man: science, labor, society. She sees as always the squalor and the grandeur. But today she sees something else as well. She sees her mission, the need of her presence. Men have need of her truths, her charity, her service and her prayer.

Oh, how many things there are to be said! But let this suffice: Understand with what genius, with what an open heart the Church of the council draws close to the modern world. The Church opens up to it not in order to be contaminated by its ways, but to infuse it with the ferment of its salvation.

Understand that from now on we must educate ourselves in this conception of the Church and of the world. Our apostolic blessing carries our wish for this renewal.

ORIGINAL SIN AND THE CHURCH'S MESSAGE OF SALVATION

BELOVED SONS AND DAUGHTERS, the mystery of original sin has very close links with the mystery of the Incarnate Word, savior of mankind through His passion, death and glorious resurrestion, and therefore also with the message of salvation entrusted to the Catholic Church.

What is the aim of the Church's pastoral action if not the redemption of human nature which, being admirably created by the all-powerful God in Adam and in him wretchedly fallen, was even more admirably recreated and regenerated by the merciful God through the grace of the only mediator Jesus Christ?

You are aware that just as the dogma of original sin was not extraneous to the drafts of constitutions of the Second Vatican Council, drafts accepted by our predecessor John XXIII of holy memory, so it was not extraneous to the Acts of the twenty-first ecumenical council.

Thus in the *Dogmatic Constitution on the Church,* in full consonance with divine revelation and the teaching of the preceding Councils of Carthage, Orange and Trent, the fact and the universality of original sin are clearly taught, as well as the intimate nature of the state from which mankind fell through Adam's guilt: "The eternal Father, by a free and hidden plan of His own wisdom and goodness, created the whole world. His plan was to raise men to a participation in the divine life. God the Father did not leave men, fallen in Adam, to themselves, but ceaselessly offered helps to salvation, in view of Christ, the Redeemer, 'who is the image of the invisible God, the firstborn of every creature'" (Col. 1:15; Dogmatic Constitution on the Church, Ch. 1, n. 2: AAS 57, 1965, pp. 5-6).

It was logical that a reference, and an even more extensive one, to the dogma of original sin should be made in the *Pastoral Constitution on the Church in the Modern World,* in which the council dealt with and fully developed the much awaited and highly important subject of the Church in the modern world.

Therefore it is not surprising that the document, referring in its introductory part to the human condition in the contemporary world, should point out the sad consequences of original sin which were already denounced in lively and effective terms by the Apostle in the letter to the Romans, although the council, following the example of St. Paul himself, does not present original sin as the sole source of mankind's ills.

It is said in fact in the constitution: "The truth is that the imbalances under which the modern world labors are linked with that more basic imbalance which is rooted in the heart of man. For in man himself many elements wrestle with one another. Hence he suffers division within himself, from which indeed arise so many and such great discords within society" (Expository introduction, n. 10). In explicit terms the constitution itself in Chapter I, referring tacitly to Genesis (Ch. 3) and the doctrine of the Council of Trent, indicates the first man's sin as the principal source of the moral disorder existing in mankind, declaring: "Although he was made by God in a state of holiness, from the very beginning of his history man abused his liberty, at the urging of the Evil One. Man set himself against God and sought to attain his goal apart from God" (Ch. I, n. 13).

The doctrine of original sin both regarding its existence and universality, its character as true sin even in the descendants of Adam and its sad consequences for soul and body, is a truth revealed by God in various passages of the Old and of the New Testament, but especially in the texts of Genesis 3:1-20, and of the Letter to the Romans, 5:12-19.

It is therefore evident that the explanations of original sin given by some modern authors are irreconcilable with true Catholic doctrine. Starting from the undemonstrated premise of polygenism, they deny, more or less clearly, that that sin committed at the beginning of history, from which so many cesspools of evil have come to mankind was first of all the disobedience of Adam, the "first man," (Second Vatican Council, Pastoral Constitution on the Church in the Modern World, n. 22; cf. also n. 13). Consequently these explanations do not even agree with the teaching of Scripture, of sacred tradition and the Church's magisterium, according to which the sin of the first man is transmitted to all his descendants not through imitation but through propagation, "in each one as his own" and is "the death of the soul," that is, privation and not simple lack of holiness and of justice even in newborn babies (cf. Council of Trent, 5th session, canon 2-3).

Even the theory of "evolutionism" is not acceptable where it is not decidedly in accord with the immediate creation of each and every human soul by God, and where it does not regard as decisively important for the fate of mankind the disobedience of Adam, universal protoparent (cf. Council of Trent, session 5, canon 2). That disobedience must not be considered as if it did not make Adam lose the holiness and justice in which he was constituted (cf. Council of Trent, session 5, canon 1).

With the intent of raising the hearts of men and enkindling their hopes, the council, together with St. Paul, points out to them in the figure of the saving Christ, founder of the Church, the new Adam whose light confirms and illustrates what happened in the first Adam and continues to happen in his progeny. "The truth is," we read in our document, "that only in the mystery of the Incarnate Word does the mystery of man take on light. For Adam, the first man, was a figure of Him who was to come (Rom. 5:14), namely Christ the Lord. Christ, the final Adam, by the revelation of the mystery of the Father and His love, fully reveals man to man himself and makes his supreme calling clear. It is not surprising, then, that in Him all the aforementioned truths find their root and attain their crown.... Such is the mystery of man, and it is a great one, as seen by believers in the light of Christian revelation. Through Christ and in Christ, the riddles of sorrow and death grow meaningful. Apart from His Gospel, they overwhelm us" (Ch. I, n. 22).

As it clearly emerges from these texts to which we considered it fitting to draw your attention, the Second Vatican Council did not aim at deepening and completing the Catholic doctrine on original sin, already sufficiently declared and defined, as we said, in the Councils of Carthage (418), of Orange (529) and of Trent (1546). It wanted only to confirm it and apply it in accordance with its predominantly pastoral purposes.

WHAT IS THE CHURCH?

BELOVED SONS AND DAUGHTERS, if in visiting you come with the attitude of a pilgrim who is not content with viewing as an outsider the exterior scene of this audience, but as one who wants to look within, to see something of the present spiritual reality, to understand and discover the sense of what he approaches and observes, you will feel arise within yourselves a clear word and an obscure question.

The clear word is: Here is the Church, the Catholic Church—not all of the Catholic Church and not only the Church, of course, but the Catholic Church in its most characteristic and authoritative expression, the Catholic Church represented by its visible head, the Catholic Church in its central See, in the cardinal point of its faith and history. Here is the tomb of the first Apostle, St. Peter. Here is his successor, the Pope. Here is evident the apostolicity, the unity, the catholicity, the constitutional sanctity of the Church, the famous "notes" which distinguish and certify it. Here is the meeting point with all Catholics throughout the world, in fact the point of ecumenical attraction of all Christians, believers in the Lord Jesus.

And so it goes. Here, you rightly say, is the Church to which you belong, the Church in its center, in its most meaningful sign, in its safest foundation. This is clear.

But then a question arises in the soul of a pilgrim, one which appears simple but is not. This very simple question is this: What is the Church?

All of you surely remember the answer of the catechism, attributed to Pius X: "The Church is the society of true Christians, in other words of those baptized who profess the faith and doctrine of Jesus Christ, who participate in its sacraments and obey the shepherds established by Him."

True, but does this definition tell us everything about the Church? This is rather a description, exact and sufficient enough to give an idea of the Church as distinguished from other societies. But, rather than satisfy us, it gives rise to a need to understand "per causas"—in other words the intrinsic reasons for this associative fact in its constituent principles—the thing so different from anything else that is called the Church. All of us would like to know something more about it.

This is so true that all those who have some knowledge of the spiritual questions of our times find that the science of the Church, "ecclesiology," is a very lively need of our times. To know what the Church is becomes a decisive matter in view of many other questions, first the religious, then the ecumenical, the humanistic, etc.

Such knowledge for us Catholics is all the more important because many errors, many incorrect ideas, many individual opinions circulate in the discussions of our times.

The interest, which now attracts the attention of those who are concerned and hope for the recomposition of the unity of the separated Christians toward a true concept of the Church, submits this theme for the study and before the conscience of the contemporary world. We must know well what the Church is, the true Church, that Church to which we have duties we cannot ignore, the Church in which we wish to find truth and salvation, without pluralisms contrary to its unitary and constitutive principle, and without elastic and equivocal uncertainties to remove from us the fortune of the univocal solution (even if varied in the contingent and external forms) of the great question.

The importance of the question grows for two reasons: first, because such a question was at the center of the Second Vatican Ecumenical Council—the principle question, the one most studied and most illustrated by doctrinal affirmations of profound context and of very high value.

Secondly, because it can be said that the council itself found it difficult to give a simple, straightforward and easy idea of the Church, in other words it found itself faced with a reality so full of significance, so great and complex, that it had to be called a mystery.

The Church is a mystery, not only in the sense of the hidden depth of its life, but also in the sense that it is a reality not so much human, historical and visible as it is divine and transcends our normal capacity of knowledge. As we see it today, the Church itself is a sign, a sacred sign, a sacrament, which we cannot now know adequately in its true and inner fullness but which attracts us now precisely to a new and stupendous study.

What shall we do then to understand something? Here if there is a study of which love also contributes toward the conquest of truth, we believe that it is the study of the Church. To know the Church well we must love it, and afterwards study it. One of the most interesting studies in this respect is the great *Dogmatic Constitution on the Church*. In it, among other things worthy of note, is the multiplicity of names given to the Church. It is designated by figures of speech and symbols, as was the custom of authors of authors of the Sacred Books who were averse to our modern practice of using abstract terms and speculative definitions.

It will be sufficient to make a list of these names to understand how the reality of the Church is vast and complex. It is called the Israel of God, the Kingdom of Heaven, the City of God, the Heavenly Jerusalem, the Bride of Christ, the Mother of the Faithful, the Field of God, the Vineyard of the Lord, the Fold of Christ, the House of God, the People of God, and lastly, the Mystical Body of Christ.

This multiplicity of names shows us that the Church can be considered under different aspects, each of which is like the light from a many-faceted diamond.

Beloved children, let yourselves be attracted by these lights. The Church is not a screen to prevent us from reaching Christ and rising toward God, as was said by many who are strangers to our indescribable communion, but is the mirror—the sacred sign—in which we must see Christ and in Him God.

May our blessing obtain for you to be all disciples of this marvelous school, which is that of the study of Holy Church.

THE CHURCH AS THE HOUSE OF GOD

BELOVED SONS AND DAUGHTERS, our weekly meeting with so many of the faithful and visitors, always new and numerous, made possible by the general audiences, turns our thought to the great subject of the Church as the most obvious, the most ample and the most beautiful subject for this moment of familiar conversation. Do not be surprised if we once more speak of her to you. We could never cease speaking of her, so important is she and so fruitful are her teachings.

Last week we mentioned the various names given to the Church in Holy Scripture. This variety shows that it is difficult to contain in one single name the exuberant wealth of the mysterious reality of the Church. It also indicates the instructive manner through which Sacred Scripture introduces us to knowledge of the Church.

Let us take one of these names, for example, the House of God. It is St. Paul who makes use of it in writing to Timothy. He says: "I write these things to you . . . in order that you may know . . . how to conduct yourself in the house of God, which is the Church of the living God, the pillar and mainstay of the truth" (1 Tim. 3:15). This image of the house, likened to the Church, calls to mind other similar images which we find in the holy books likewise refer to the Church.

Once again, St. Paul will say of Christians: "You are God's building" (1 Cor. 3:9). The thought applies to the words of Jesus Himself: "I will build my Church" (Matt. 16:18). It applies to the cornerstone (Matt. 21:42) which is Christ Himself who upholds the entire construction. And it applies to Simon, whose name Jesus changed to Peter so that it might in some manner be likened to Christ, his visible vicar as we say, in the function of foundation and support of the edifice of which Christ says He wishes to be the builder, the architect, the artist.

To what doctrinal concepts does this image of the Church as the house of God direct us? This is difficult to say in a few words; but each of you may find them, almost by yourself. For example, is not the house a dwelling? Does it not indicate an inner experience? Is it not a dwelling place where a family comes together? Does it not spell an inner unity, an intimacy lived and protected?

Does not the image of a house, applied to many persons, teach us that such a plurality should make for a community? Does it not teach us also that it should be unity in love, in harmony, in the identity of thoughts and sentiments? How could the Church of Christ, conceived as the house of God, be otherwise?

And if such a house is not simply destined to gather together the official ecclesial society that inhabits it, but is destined to make possible, to provoke in a certain way, the meeting of the fortunate residents with God, then that house appears to us as sacred, it becomes a temple, and it shows us how the Church is a true and necessary place to communicate with God.

Likewise it shows us that it is the focal point of His light. It is the place where He awaits us, where He grants Himself to us, where we can speak trustingly with Him, where we can enjoy His presence, where we can live the "mystery" of the relationship instituted by Christ between God and man. In the Church we become—"members of God's household" (Eph. 2:19).

It would be sufficient to meditate over this concept of the Church as the House of God to have a source of endless thoughts: Where is the pluralism that some would like to attribute to the unique Church; where is the outward aspect for which others would like to reproach the visible Church; without mentioning that such cohesion in structure gives us the starting point for many other considerations. The Church is a construction in the making; it is not yet a finished construction, it is on the way to being completed.

Does not this aspect speak to us of the common image of the history of the Church, of her development promoted by Christ, the true builder of His Church, through the action of the Holy Spirit? Does it not speak to us of her present unfinished state, of her continuous growth, of her beauty which is revealed as the construction proceeds, in other words, as the centuries pass?

Does not this image remind us of the perennial character of the Church, of her faithfulness to doctrinal and structural foundations, of her truth, the same today as yesterday and tomorrow, though always responsive to a deepening, in fact an elevating identification of the contents and a prodigious freshness of expression?

Try, beloved children, to think of the Church as the house of God. You will find there the answer to many misinterpretations that distort her concept. You will find there the invitation to step more deeply into that blessed house, to know her better, to dwell there with joy and dignity. You will find there the discovery of a great fortune, precisely that of having a home, a home where love of your brethren is the principle for dwelling together and where God's love for us and our love for God find their happiest and most promising celebration.

Our apostolic blessing exhorts you to the above.

THE MARVEL OF THE CHURCH

BELOVED SONS AND DAUGHTERS, we know that we are speaking to thousands of students and we hope that their visit to the Pope might leave in them a special memory—not only a memory of the scene now before your eyes, the scene of this basilica filled with people, around this altar under which is the tomb of St. Peter. Peter, the Apostle whose name was Simon (son of John) and whom Jesus wished especially that he be called instead Peter to signify that he was to be the foundation, was the rock on which Jesus wished to build an edifice, the edifice called the Church. We hope that this audience may imprint in our visitors, and particularly in these children, the memory of the Church.

What is the Church? How do you imagine her? We said an edifice; in fact, the name "church" serves to indicate the holy edifice where we go to pray. However, it also serves to indicate society, people, those who go to church. It indicates, in other words, the community of persons who believe in Christ, and who together form a group, a multitude—united, orderly, concordant, good, religious, happy, and completely moved by great thoughts and great hopes. This is the Church, as all of you well know.

Now we ask you: is there an image, in addition to that of the edifice that represents the Church, precisely in its aspect of a multitude gathered around a center? Yes, it is an image that Jesus Himself left with us; an image which you will often hear repeated, that of the flock gathered around its shepherd, a flock guided, known, and defended by its shepherd.

He Himself said it, "I am the good Shepherd" (John 10:14); in other words, the only Shepherd, the Shepherd who alone knows how to guide, the Shepherd who sacrifices Himself to defend and save His flock.

And what does the flock mean? It means humanity, it means the world, it means us, we ourselves. This image says less to us moderns than it did to the ancient people who were used more than we to look upon the rural scene of the shepherd who leads his flock to pasture. It was an image which was dear to the language of the past. Once kings were called the shepherds of the people (cf. Homer). The prophets had announced the Messiah as shepherd of Israel.

It is nevertheless an image so simple and beautiful that it can also serve to signify for us the gathering of many followers, held together and led by a single head, by a single guide. That is to say, men, the faithful, who find in Jesus Christ the principle of their unity and form a social body around Him. This is the Church.

Jesus who at first had given to Simon the name of Peter, at the end of the Gospel in the famous and marvelous scene on the shores of the lake of Tiberias gives to Peter himself the function of Shepherd. Three times He asks him to be the shepherd of His sheepfold ("feed my lambs; feed my sheep" John 21:15-17); that is to say, Jesus entrusts to Simon Peter the task Jesus had declared to be His own. He names Simon Peter His successor, His vicar, His representative.

If you were able to read the large words written in mosaic on the gold band under the large cornice of this basilica, in Latin and Greek, you would find the pronouncements of Jesus who invests Peter with his functions: "Feed my lambs, feed my sheep." In other words you would see recalled through the very expressions of Christ, the figure of the Church, symbolized in the shepherd and in the flock.

This figure, this similitude, this is the memory we hoped would remain in your minds following this audience, which for you is a characteristic meeting with Holy Church, to which all of you belong.

What does the figure of the shepherd and of the flock, referred to the Church, teach us? It teaches us two qualities of the Church which must be very dear to us and which aid us in understanding many things relating to the world, to history, to our life: unity and Catholicity.

The Church is unique and universal. She is a marvelous thing. If you will study, if you will travel, you will understand something of this most simple and sublime design of God for the salvation of humanity.

This figure also teaches us that this universal unity which was founded by Christ and which is being realized in the course of time, is held together by two principal forces, similarity of thought and mutual affection.

Let us explain it better: by faith, equal for all, and by love—not by force, not for advantage, not for laziness—but by Christ's love for us and by our love for Christ and for our fellowmen whom we call brothers. This is the Church!

Will you remember this? Will you always try to remain faithful and loving to the Church? Will you be happy to be Catholics? Certainly, with our apostolic blessing.

THE DESIGN OF THE DIVINE FOUNDER

BELOVED SONS AND DAUGHTERS, at these weekly meetings, these general audiences, we want to speak of the Church: the ecumenical council offers us ample subject matter, thereof, and indeed almost makes it an obligation for us, due to the abundance and the authority of the doctrine regarding the Church herself which it has illustrated to us.

Your visit lends us the opportunity to make some mention of such doctrine, without claiming to deal with it or expound it adequately, but only with the aim and the pleasure of fleetingly pointing out some aspect worthy of special consideration.

And do you know which, in our opinion, is the most interesting, and at the same time, most mysterious, aspect of the doctrine regarding the Church? It is that which refers to the relationship between the Church and the Holy Spirit.

The council says, in an admirable and compact page of theology: "I have accomplished the work that thou hast given me to do" (cf. John 17:14); on the day of Pentecost the Holy Spirit was sent to continually sanctify the Church in order that believers might through Christ have access in one Spirit to the Father" (cf. Eph. 2:18).

He is the Spirit Who gives life; He is a fountain of water, springing up into life everlasting (cf. John 4:14; 7:38-39); through Him the Father restores life to men dead through sin, until one day He will bring their mortal bodies to life in Christ (cf. Rom. 8:10-11).

The Spirit dwells in the Church and in the hearts of the faithful as in a temple (cf. 1 Cor. 3:16; 6:19) and in them prays and gives evidence of their filial adoption (cf. Gal. 4:6; Rom. 8:15-16 and 26). He guides the Church toward all of the truth (cf. John 16:13). He unifies her in communion and in the ministry, He instructs and directs her with different hierarchic and charismatic gifts and embellishes her with His fruits (cf. Eph. 4:11-12; 1 Cor. 12:4; Gal. 5:22).

By virtue of the Gospel the Holy Spirit rejuvenates the Church, continually renews her and leads her to a perfect union with her Spouse, because the Spirit and the Spouse say to the Lord Jesus: Come (cf. Apoc. 22:17).

It is a lengthy page, filled with biblical references, which would normally require an explanation. We here, however, simply to outline the relationship between the Holy Spirit and the Church, are content with quoting a phrase of a great German Catholic thinker of the past century who, on the front page of a famous book of his on unity in the Church, writes with concise vigor: "the Father sends the Son and the Son sends the Holy Spirit. It is thus that God has come to us. It is in an inverted sense that we arrive at the Father. The Spirit leads us to the Son, and the Son to the Father" (Moehler).

It will be sufficient for us to think of the Holy Spirit as the divine principle animator of the Church, as her uncreated soul (cf. Journet 1, 43, 665), that produces in the Mystical Body of the Lord the created animation, in other words, the grace, the gifts of the Holy Spirit, the fruits of the Holy Spirit (Gal. 5:22), which St. Paul enumerates thus: "charity, joy, peace, patience, kindness, goodness, forebearance, meekness, faith, moderation, continence, and chastity."

Furthermore, is not the sacramental character an effect of the Holy Spirit? Likewise His inspirations that guide souls on the way to sanctity? And is not the aid of the Holy Spirit, which lends to the ministry of the Church its orientation and security, also the work of the Holy Spirit?

A point of special importance in all this marvelous doctrine is that which relates to the hierarchy of the Church.

Is not the Holy Spirit perhaps free to exercise His mysterious action directly? "The wind blows where it will" (John 3:8). Of course; the council affirms this expressly and repeatedly (cf. Dogmatic Constitution on the Church, n. 12-16; Unitatis redintegratio, 3, 4, 21, etc.).

Therefore, the service which the Church intends to provide in teaching, sanctifying, and guiding the faithful—is it not superfluous and cumbersome? Do not the faithful receive the Holy Spirit directly, without this human screen, this intermediary institution?

This is an essential point of the Church's doctrine. We must have recourse to Christ's thinking. Christ entrusted the fulfillment of His work among men to two different factors: the Holy Spirit and the Apostles. He promised to send the Holy Spirit and He sent the Apostles.

These two missions come equally from Christ. The indisputable design of the Divine Founder of the Church intends that the Church be built by the Apostles and vivified by the Holy Spirit. The Apostles build the body of the Church, whose soul is the Spirit of Christ. These two different agents are so linked to each other that St. Augustine, in his famous and incisive words, affirms that the work of one is the extension of the other: "Nothing participates in the Spirit of Christ except the Body of Christ. . . . Do you wish therefore to find life in the Spirit of Christ? Then be in the Body of Christ" (Tract on John the Evangelist 26, 13; P.L. 35, 1612-1613).

And again: "The Christian need fear nothing so much as to be separated from the Body of Christ. If in fact he is separated from the Body of Christ, he is not His member; and if he is not His member, he is not nourished by His Spirit" (ib. Tract 27, 6; P.L. 35, 1618).

We should always remember how the work of the visible hierarchy is concerned with the diffusion of the Holy Spirit among the members of the Church. Its ministry is not indispensable to the operation of God's mercy, which may be diffused as God pleases. But it is normally indispensable for us who have the mandate and good fortune of having received the word of God, the grace of God, the guidance of God from the Apostles, that is to say "from the ministers of the religious supernatural life emanating from Christ" (cf. Congar, *Esquisses du mystere de l'eglise,* p. 129 ss.).

We like to remember these shining truths at the eve of the beginning of the novena, the great novena of Pentecost. We wished that the celebration of this "metropolis of feasts," as St. John Chrysostom calls Pentecost, were preceded by the preparation which the Lord Himself instituted (cf. Acts 1:4; 12; 2:1), in gathering together, in prayer, in meditation on the mystery of the Church, not only in its inner depths, but also in its external manifestations: it is an infinite meditation.

We should like the beautiful encyclical of Leo XIII, *Divinum Illud Munus* (1897), to be recalled and understood. We should like worship and love of the Holy Spirit to be more fervent and more widespread among Christians. This is what we recommend to you for your good and for that of the whole Church, with our apostolic blessing.

A PERMANENT MIRACLE

BELOVED SONS AND DAUGHTERS, permit us, out of the fatherhood of our ministry, to put a question to you: How did you celebrate the feast of Pentecost?

Did you try to understand how the prodigious event, told in the Acts of the Apostles (Ch. 2), stands at the very beginning of the Church, not only as an important historical fact, but also as a vital principle? How it stands as the beginning of the supernatural enlivening of the Church, as the spring of a permanent miracle—that of the infusion of the Holy Spirit in the Apostles and in believers in relation to Christ's formation in their individual lives, and in the entire community, united though internally differentiated and hierarchical, which is called the Church?

Have you thought how the fact continues on, stretches itself throughout time, extends over the earth, wherever faith and grace reach, and profoundly concerns each one of us?

Have you thought how the effusion of the Holy Spirit has reached your individual souls and penetrated into the internal round of your psychology and ignited therein the divine life?

One of the most mysterious and most marvelous pages of our catechism is precisely that which relates to the communication of the Holy Spirit to the faithful, bringing about in them a new state—a state of grace with all the successive operative attitudes, with all the infused virtues, and with all the spiritual gifts and fruits with which this divine enlivenment enriches the souls that have the invaluable good fortune of being pervaded by the enlivening and sanctifying Love.

It is a difficult page, because it deals with truths which go beyond our human science and which ordinarily are not perceivable by our experience, unless through some inner reflection which conscience senses more or less clearly, but always with intimate joy and with a characteristic breath of peace, the peace of Christian conscience.

This however is a page with which we must become acquainted and which the council has repeatedly made evident.

The Holy Spirit has had a place of honor, the one which pertains to Him in the council documents. We need to give only one quotation here: There having been accomplished the work that the Father had given the Son to do on earth (cf. John 17:4), there was sent on the day of Pentecost the Holy Spirit to continually sanctify the Church, and so that believers might thus have access to the Father through Christ in one sole Spirit (cf. Eph. 2:18).

He is the Spirit Who gives life; He is a fountain of water springing up unto life everlasting (cf. John 4:14; 7:38-39). Through Him the Father restores life to men, dead by reason of sin, until one day their mortal bodies will be brought to life in Christ (cf. Rom. 8:10-11). The Spirit dwells in the Church and in the hearts of the faithful as in a temple (cf. 1 Cor. 3:16; 6:19) and prays in them and gives testimony of their filial adoption (cf. Gal. 4: 6; Rom. 8: 15-16 and 26).

He guides the Church throughout all the truth (cf. John 16:13), unifies the Church in the communion and ministry, instructs and directs her with different hierarchical and charismatic gifts, and embellishes her with His fruits (cf. Eph. 4:11-12; 1 Cor. 12-4; Gal. 5:22).

By the power of the Gospel He makes the Church grow, perpetually renews her and leads her to perfect union with (Christ) her Spouse. The Spirit and the Bride both say to the Lord Jesus, 'Come,'" (cf. Apoc. 22:17).

Thus the Church shines forth as "a people made one with the unity of the Father, the Son, and the Holy Spirit" (Dogmatic Constitution on the Church, n. 4).

From this marvelous doctrinal synthesis we can draw two single, important conclusions. The first regards the relationships of our soul with the Holy Spirit, the worship, in other words, which we must cultivate in the hidden recesses of our heart and in the expression of prayer, with this ineffable "sweet guest of the soul." This is a worship which begins with an inner sense of sacredness which every Christian, made a temple of the Holy Spirit by Baptism (cf. 1 Cor. 3:16), should himself develop with the refining of the conscience, as a result of which "how bitterly the slightest fault doth sting thee!" (transl. by Lawrence Grant White—Dante's Purg. 3:9), and to which one thing matters above all others: to be in the grace of God, to be vigilant in love and in faithfulness to God present.

It is a worship that recognizes in the Holy Spirit the principle of prayer, thereby gaining for us from Him the blessed possibility of proffering the name of Jesus (1 Cor. 12:3) and the mystical spring of the most moving prayer (Rom. 8:26) and which acknowledges to Him, as though He had passed over His Church, the liturgical renewal of our times (Sacr. Concilium 43).

Among all, our first devotion should be to the Holy Spirit.

The next conclusion regards our relationship with the Church, intended as a visible and hierarchical, dogmatic, sacramental and canonical society.

There are those who are tempted to regard this external ecclesial relationship as extraneous and superfluous, as if it were contrary and almost abusive in relation to the intimate "charismatic" relationship of the soul with the Holy Spirit.

Let us be cautious, beloved sons, regarding this problem and let us try to solve it properly. The Church, the Mystical Body of Christ, does not distinguish herself from the socially organized Church who confers on us our title of Catholic, who gives to our souls sanctified by grace the very form of the new Christian life, and who is the indispensable instrument whereby we have the doctrine, the sacraments and the guidance which lead us to, and preserve us in, communion with the Holy Spirit.

Yes, let us open the sail of the soul to the wind of the Spirit of Jesus, which blows where it will (John 3:8), free and mysterious.

But let us not surrender the rudder of the apostolic Fisherman, who governs us for a good purpose.

May our apostolic blessing be with you together with this simple counseling.

THE CHURCH IS LIKE A CITY

BELOVED SONS AND DAUGHTERS, again we shall speak to you of the Church. It is the subject that presents itself most easily at an encounter such as a general audience. Then again it has been made a matter of interest by the ecumenical council. It was the principal topic of the council's discussions and deliberations. It is the recurrent subject of many studies and many comments in contemporary culture.

Our concern here is to arouse our visitors' interest in this subject, without pretending to give an organic and complete notion of it. Rather, we shall content ourselves with noting how difficult it is to say everything and to say it well about the Church, so fecund is her reality and so profound is her truth.

In fact we have said at previous general audiences that the many allegorical titles given to the Church, the many figures which try to portray the idea of the Church, show on the one hand the difficulty of defining her in words and in adequate concepts, and on the other hand the variety—interesting and inviting to meditate on and to admire—of her manifold aspects.

Let us take one of these figures of the Church from the many mentioned in the splendid conciliar *Constitution on the Church* itself: the figure of the city. The Church is like a city, a "civitas." And what is a city? Even before being an inhabited place, a group of houses, an "urbs," the city is a union of individuals, families, tribes and human groups kept close together to form a society which its laws and its own authority render homogeneous and autonomous. It is a community united and governed by a distinct social law. We can call it a nation if we consider its ethnic, historical and linguistic elements; a state if we consider it under its juridical aspect.

The Church is precisely a juridical, organized, visible and perfect society.

Let us remember the classic definition of St. Robert Bellarmine: The Church is "the assembly of men who profess the same Christian faith; it is held together by the communion of the same sacraments, under the guidance of the legitimate pastors and especially of the Roman pontiff" (*Contro.* III; de Eccl. II).

"That the Church has the form of a society is a fact obvious to all; indeed, obvious to all is the existence of a multitude of faithful Catholics, congregated (as said from the very first days of Christianity in the Didache, XI, 5) from the four winds, subject and obedient to the guidance of a supreme pastor and of other particular governors, provided with spiritual as well as temporal means destined to benefit the community and aiming at the supernatural goal of the beatific vision" (Ottaviani, *Compendium Juris* eccl. 94; Rampolla, *La Citta sul Monte*).

This is what the Lord wanted His Church to be: a true, organized, visible, religious society, with powers proper to a perfect and sovereign society, with her own laws, her own authority, her own means and ends.

This is a fundamental truth of Catholic doctrine, having firm, clear roots in the New Testament and manifest reality in the Church's history. But perhaps precisely because of this incontestable manifestation in tradition, it is one of the truths most argued and combatted in the great controversy over the Church's true nature.

Some would like her to be purely spiritual and therefore invisible, alleging that only such a Church can be of divine origin and disregarding the logical consequence that an invisible Church is no longer a Church at all (cf. Boyer, quoted by De Lubac, *Med.*, p. 68).

Even in the first century of Christianity, the holy, ringing voice of the martyr St. Ignatius of Antioch sounds the apologia of the levels of the primitive ecclesiastical hierarchy, bishop, presbyters, deacons: "Without these one cannot speak of a Church" (ad Trall. III, 1).

Then there are some who would oppose the juridical Church to the Church of charity, thinking it possible and not realizing that it is contrary to the economy of the Incarnation to isolate one constituent aspect of the Church from another, as we were forewarned by Pope Pius XII's famous encyclical on the Mystical Body (n. 62).

Certainly, the conception of the Church as a "civitas," as a society having particular forms, rights and customs, that is to say, having a human likeness, concrete and historically identified, poses many questions, first of all that of the faults which such a realization of the Church may present. But we must remember that such a conception, that is to say such a society composed of men such as we are, weak sinners in need of forgiveness and redemption, has sprung from God's goodness, from Christ's love for mankind. By gathering this society together and organizing it, Christ makes it His own, instructs it, guides it and sanctifies it, that is to say, He communicates His redemption and salvation to it through the Church.

Without considering, for the time being, other questions concerning the juridical concept of the Church, let us try to understand the grace which the Lord has granted us of being citizens of this blessed city, where an authority with divine powers gives us proof of the inexhaustible mercy of the Lord, gives us the security of His perennial sanctifying action, gives us continually a spur to the effective exercise of faith and charity, and promises us that the city itself will become transformed from the earthly to the heavenly, which is and will be the City of God, here in time, on an earth already holy in its design and in its powers but being purified and sanctified in its acts and members. One day it will be radiant and glorious, like the holy Jerusalem which John saw in the Apocalypse, "having the glory of God" (21:11).

May God grant it: with our apostolic blessing.

ONE BODY IN CHRIST

BELOVED SONS AND DAUGHTERS, to our visitors we continually repeat, especially since the ecumenical council, and today we repeat to you also the question: Do you know what the Church is?

A hundred answers rise immediately to the lips. But we ask again: Have you understood well the significance not only of this word "Church," which means assembly, meeting and society, but also the reality pointed out by this word?

In fact, what is the Church? We ask you this question because it seems to us that no moment and no place are more propitious than here and now not only to make this question rise in the minds of all those present but also to give to the question a true, full answer. What is the Church?

We will say at once that those who do not immediately perceive the difficulty of giving an adequate answer to the question lack perception. And the difficulty grows—take care!—as the Church is gradually better known, because we realize that we are not in a position to know everything about the Church. In her profound reality there is something which escapes the measure of our understanding. The Church is a mystery because she is the work of God, because she is moved by the action of the Holy Spirit, and because she is not a society consisting only of the men of this earth but also of the souls of the deceased faithful and the saints in heaven.

Yes, she is a mystery. The council repeated it. But shall we, then, never be able to form a concept, if not adequate at least in keeping with the true, essential reality of the Church?

Yes, we can and indeed we must. We know that the Church is called by various names. We have already recalled some of them. And which is the one most frequently used, the one that comes closest to truth? You certainly know it already, partly because there has been much talk about it in these past years since 1943 when Pius XII published a great encyclical which is like a treatise on the Church and was entitled the encyclical on the Mystical Body.

The Church is the Mystical Body of Christ. It was St. Paul who gave this definition and made use of it more than once in his letter: The body of Christ, he wrote, "which is the Church" (Col. 1:24). Christ, he said, "is the head of the body of the Church" (Col. 1:18). He added: "we, the many, are one body in Christ" (Rom. 12:5). There are others. We shall not detain ourselves to comment on this famous and fruitful expression except to ask another question: What did St. Paul mean when he compared the Church to a body, to a living, single organized being having Christ as her head?

If we explore this question a little we arrive at another essential title, full of meaning, which is given to the Church. It is a title we know and on which we shall now dwell. The Church is a communion (cf. Hamer). What does "communion" mean in this case? We refer you to the paragraph of the catechism which speaks of the communion of saints. The Church means the communion of saints. And the communion of saints means a two-fold vital participation: the incorporation of Christians in the life of Christ and the circulation of the same charity within the whole body of the faithful in this world and in the next; union with Christ and in Christ, and union among the Christians in the church (cf. Piolanti: *The Mystery of the Communion of the Saints*, p. 357).

A difficult doctrine? A stupendous doctrine!

A speculative doctrine? A living doctrine!

Yes, a living doctrine which should be alive in the Christian people. Perhaps we still lack an adequate understanding of this capital teaching of the Church. Did we ever really give it our attention? We are truly living in Christ (and this is why participation in the eucharistic mystery is called communion) and we are really members of the same social and spiritual organism which we call the Church. And perhaps we still lack a little pedagogy, a formation which would make us accustomed to this and make us act as the parts, as the cells, as the sons and the brothers of this ecclesial community.

What is our capacity of "loving our neighbors like ourselves"? What is our capacity for concord, for forgiving offenses, for renouncing jealousies, quarrels, discriminations, the selfishness of nationality, of language, of class, of race, of economic interests? What is the Christian genius if not that of concord, of union, of peace, of generosity, of charity? The Church is a body: the Church is communion.

Most beloved sons, may meditation on the Church make you discover her inner need for unity, for communion, and may she enable you to foretaste the inner truth of the well known words of the Psalm: "How good and how pleasant it is for brothers to dwell together in unity" (Ps. 132, 1). May our apostolic blessing obtain this for you.

THE CHURCH—BRIDE OF CHRIST AND MOTHER OF CHRISTIANS

BELOVED SONS AND DAUGHTERS, our desire to offer participants in these general audiences a thought on the Church, just as once—and perhaps even now—visitors to the most famous and sacred places tried to take away a fragment to remind them of that place and that visit, makes us dwell once more on the images through which Holy Scripture reveals to us something of the Church and helps us to think of the Church herself as of a beloved and familiar reality.

Well, today we invite you to think of the Church as if you saw her through a transparent crystal of two well known but always singular figures: the Church as the mystical bride of Christ and the Church as the mother of Christians. May these names, noble but strange—the first particularly so—help you to reflect on and to understand something of the doctrine, so vast and profound, about the Church, which we certainly do not claim to expound in these friendly conversations.

Why is the Church called a bride, the bride of Christ of course? The use of this appellation is linked to the Jewish people and goes back to the Old Testament in which the relationship between God and His people is often symbolized in nuptial love. It is good to remember that in the Old Testament God affirms Himself as the transcendent Creator—yes, the demanding lawmaker and the severe judge—but also reveals Himself as an always vigilant and most tender love, a solicitous and gratuitous love, a faithful and merciful love, a sweet and inebriating love; a love that chastises, forgives and saves, and so on (cf. Jer. 2:2; Osea 6:6; Is. 49:15; Ez. 16:59-63).

In the New Testament the image of the bridegroom is referred by the precursor to Jesus (John 3:28-29 and cf. in the parables: Mt. 22:2-14; Mt. 25:1-13). He Himself compares Himself at one time to a bridegroom who gladdens his guests (Mt. 9:14). But it is again St. Paul who gives the image its most precise ecclesiological significance in the famous passage of the letter to the Ephesians: "Christ has loved the Church . . ." (Eph. 5:21-32); an image which will be carried by the Apocalypse into eternal glory, allowing us to perceive in the nuptials of the Lamb the blessed union of Christ with redeemed mankind invested with the title and the dignity of His mystical bride (Apoc. 19:7-9; cf. Vonier, "*L'Esprit et L'Epouse,*" p. 48 Ed. Cerf 1947).

What does this allegory, authorizing us to call the Church the bride of Christ, teach us? It teaches us the love surpassing all love which Christ had for the Church, a love which can in a way be signified by human marriage but is more substantial and profound than this. Let the theologians, let the mystics say what union there is between Christ and mankind, deriving from the Incarnation—"a marital union," wrote St. Augustine, "Verbum et caro," PL 36, 495—and deriving from the sacrifice of Redemption: Christ "delivered Himself up for her" (Eph. 5:25).

It has often been said that the Church is a mystery. Yes, but now we may at least know what this mystery is. It is a mystery of charity, of falling in love with God through Christ and in the Holy Spirit, of the world of mankind, that is to say of the Church. The epigraph of the Church can well be:—"thus God loved" (John 3:16); "for too much love" (Eph. 2:4); or "Christ loved us" (Eph. 5:2; 2 Thess. 2:15) and so on.

It teaches us the intimate and indissoluble union and at the same time the distinction between Christ and the Church. It teaches us that the Church is neither a beginning nor an end in herself. She belongs to Christ. From Him the Church receives her dignity, her sanctifying virtue, her lowly and sublime royalty. It teaches us that the Church is not only the instrument of salvation but the terminal of salvation because in her the design and the charity of the Lord terminate. The apotheosis is celebrated in her of victorious mankind in heaven (cf. Hymn of Dedication: "Sposaeque ritu cingeris. . .").

Let them think of this who have nothing for the Church but critical or hostile judgments. Let them think of this who regard her as a useless baffle between man and God and do not remember that she is the point of encounter of Christ's love for us; the nuptial abode, that is to say the Holy Church. "Holy Church is the nuptial abode," said St. Gregory the Great (Hom. 38; PL 76, 1287).

Well, then, thinking of this need which we have of the Church, the other image follows the first. The

Church is our mother. To her we owe everything. She generated us to a new life, the life of grace which will give us our eternal happiness. She has given us the faith, and with her magisterium preserves it for us unequivocal, integral and fecund. She has given us grace. She is the dispenser of the sacraments. She has given us charity, the "agape," the society of our brothers. She unites us, she educates us to love, to true humanism, to the understanding and the edification of her. She guides us, she defends us, she marshalls us on the paths of hope, she foreshadows for us the eschatological desire for the future life and makes us foretaste its happiness. By her magisterium, by her ministry, "every Christian is sustained in an effective manner in the gift of himself to Christ; by means of the network she is weaving, each finds himself truly linked with all his brothers; by means of the human voice that teaches and commands, each listens still to the voice of his Lord" (cf. De Lubac, Medit. 205).

The words of St. Ambrose come to mind: "Mater ergo viventium Ecclesia est" (PL 5, 1585)—the Church is the mother of living men. We must think of it, beloved sons. We must rejoice in it. We must envy the dying St. Catherine for the final words of her flaming life: "In truth, I have consumed and given my life in the Church and for the Holy Church; which is for me a most singular grace" (Joergensen 518-519).

And thus we, and thus you, most beloved sons. With our apostolic blessing.

THE CHURCH—LIGHT OF ALL MANKIND

BELOVED SONS AND DAUGHTERS, in these weekly talks, we seek to understand something of the great and profound doctrine which the recent Ecumenical Council has proclaimed in reference to holy Church and which will in the future engage the study, prayer and activity of the Church herself.

We are satisfied here at this See, to quote the names, titles and images by which the Church is called. And it seems to us that every nominal expression which holy Scripture and the council refer to the Church seems almost a flash of light, a revelation, an opening toward some better understanding of the great truth—in fact of the great reality which our holy and blessed Church of God is.

"As the Lord," St. John Chrysostom says, "so also the Church is called by many names" (Hom. de capto Eutropio, PG. latine 28, 402).

Will you today focus for an instant your attention on a title, one marvelous, shining, though dazzling by its very light, which the council has attributed to the Church? The title is: light of all mankind, in other words, beacon of all nations, light of peoples.

It is with this expression, “light of nations,” that the Second Vatican Council's *Dogmatic Constitution on the Church* starts and is thus entitled—surely the most important document which the Council issued. The Church is called the light of all mankind.

Where does this name come from? It was Pope John XXIII, of hallowed memory, who applied it to the Church, exactly because of the fact that he called the Church to the council.

In the radio message which our beloved predecessor launched to the world one month before the opening of the council, on September 11, 1962, he applied to the Church the acclamation which the liturgy of Holy Saturday applies to the newly lighted paschal candle, the symbol of the risen Christ, which brings the consolation of brightness and hope to the community of the faithful enveloped in the darkness of night.

Pope John XXIII said at that time: “It appears to us here to be proper and good to refer to the symbolism of the paschal candle. At a point of the liturgy, its name resounds: Lumen Christi. The Church of Jesus from all points of the earth replies: *Deo gratias. Deo gratias*, as if saying: yes, *lumen Christi; lumen Ecclesia; lumen gentium*” (*Discourses* . . . 1962, p. 521, 527).

This single expression of light, referred to God's revelation, to the chosen people and afterwards to the Word Incarnate—to Christ, in relation to the salvation of the world—would deserve endless study (cf. Is. 42:6; 49:6; 60:1; Acts 13:47; John 1:5; etc).

What is of interest to us is the twofold passage of the light of the world, which is Christ, first to the

Church, afterwards from the Church to the world. All of us recall the sublime words of Jesus: "I am the light of the world; he who follows me does not walk in the darkness, but will have the light of life (John 8:12); words which are afterwards repeated: "As long as I am in the world, I am the light of the world" (John 9:5); "I have come as a light into the world, that whoever believes in me may not remain in the darkness" (John 12:46).

Therefore Christ is the source of light; He is the light.

But how does this light reach us?

The Lord wished to establish a system, to provide an order so that His light would reach us through a human service, through a qualified and authorized reflex, in other words, through the apostolic teaching authority and ministry. He, in fact, said to the apostles: "You are the light of the world" (Matt. 5:14).

And again, through an inner transparence of Christ Himself, emanating from the entire mystical and visible body of the Church, as though the Church were the monstrance of Christ; thus she herself is called a "sacrament," that is to say, the sacred sign and course of God's union with humanity (cf. Dogmatic Constitution on the Church, n. 1).

"He who hears you," Jesus said in referring to the disciples raised to hierarchical duties, "hears me; and he who rejects you, rejects me" (Luke 10:16). In practice, therefore, we could not arrive at Christ, unless we sought Him and found Him in His Church. We still recall the famous exhortation of St. John Chrysostom: "Do not estrange yourself from the Church! Nothing is stronger than she! The Church is your hope, the Church is your refuge. She is higher than heaven and more vast than the earth. She never grows old, but thrives always" (ibid.).

Another great Eastern doctor, Origen, back in the first half of the third century, in commenting on Genesis, said: "If we too wish to be like heaven, we will have in us the lights that can enlighten us: Christ and His Church. He in fact is the light of the world, that enlightens also the Church by His light; . . . and the Church, having taken the light of Christ, enlightens all those who find themselves in the darkness of ignorance" (In Gen. Hom. 1, 5; PG 12, 150).

From this there derives another fact: the Church reflects the light of Christ over the world. The council says that the countenance of the Church is so luminous that the world is brightened (Constitution on the Church, n. 1).

How does this fact occur? It happens through the proclamation of the Gospel, we know. But it occurs also in another way, by the external illumination of certain qualities, of certain notes, which derive from essential and intrinsic properties of the Church, and which, to the eyes of the world, give evidence of her authenticity.

These are the four famous characteristic and exclusive marks of the Church—you know them—her apostolicity, unity, catholicity and sanctity. They are proclaimed in the Creed as distinctive of the countenance of the true Church. She carries in herself and spreads around her the explanation of her very self.

Those who look at the Church, those who study her with a loving eye for truth, cannot but acknowledge that she—independently of the people who form her, and from the practical ways with which she presents herself—carries in herself a message of universal and single light, one liberating, necessary and divine. The Church is the laborious and victorious discovery, to quote a great and typical example of Newman (cf. Denz. Schoenm., 2888).

This carries a reminder, beloved sons, that to each of us (faithful) is given both power and duty to emphasize these marks which form the beauty and the magnetism of the Church, showing by our adherence and our witness how truly the Church of Christ is one, holy, catholic, apostolic.

May our apostolic blessing exhort and enable you to receive and spread this "Light of nations."

THE CHURCH CARRIES CHRIST THROUGH TIME

BELOVED SONS AND DAUGHTERS: you, too, like all those—whether in or outside the Church—who were moved by the great event which was the ecumenical council to reflect upon the nature and mission of the Church, may have asked yourselves: Essentially, what does the Church do? What, exactly, is her activity?

These questions, though quite important and interesting, find ready answers.

It is evident that the Church lives and acts to continue and spread Christ's mission. The fundamental conception, on which the entire doctrine concerning the Church is based, is the notion of continuation.

The Church is the prolongation and development of the Gospel. The Church carries Christ through time, through centuries, through history, and advances toward the final eschatological meeting with Christ in His glory.

A word of God reassures it: "I am with you all days, even unto the consummation of the world" (Matt. 28:20).

However, this continuation is not purely static, immobile, conservative. The Church is not an organization closed within itself, and solicitous only to defend and preserve itself. The Church was born to bear witness: "You," the Lord said to the Apostles before leaving them, "shall be witnesses for me . . . even to the very ends of the earth" (Acts 1:8).

The Church is destined to cover the earth; she is instituted for all of humanity; she is universal, therefore catholic.

We must reflect well upon this inborn vocation of the Church, and remember that the Lord wished us to think of the Church as a seed which by its very nature must germinate, expand and bear fruit; or, as a ferment which raises, swells and infuses flavor into the mass.

The Church is apostolic by her very nature; that is to say, missionary. What we mean is that the Church is always active and altogether engaged in an effort to spread her message of salvation, her concept of life and of the world, and her Gospel.

What, then, does the Church do?

It is evident: She speaks, preaches, instills, spreads, proclaims the doctrine of Christ. She preaches on the housetops, what has been confided to her ears (Matt. 10:28).

The Church, there where she is alive, understood, faithful to the mandate of Christ, has a first and indispensable activity: that of announcing the divine word.

The faith, as the root of all the doctrinal and moral system of Christianity, requires such announcement, demands such preaching. "The faith then," St. Paul says, "depends on hearing" (Rom. 10:17).

The catechesis—a catechesis exact, faithful, orthodox, one not arbitrary, not changeable—is her first duty.

The liturgy of the word precedes the eucharistic liturgy. The Church is the continuous, exact and authoritative echo of God's teachings. The Church is an apostolate, a school, a "propagation of the faith," an effort which extends to obstinacy. Do you recall the Apostles?—"For we cannot but speak" (Acts 4:20)—which extends to sacrifice. Do you recall Stephen? And what are the martyrs, if not preachers, witnesses to the Gospel, with blood?

We would never end these simple considerations if, with quotations from council texts, we sought to substantiate how and to what extent the Church, in the great act of reflection accomplished over her in the solemn Vatican Synod, has confirmed and expressed this basic mission of hers: of being apostolic, of being missionary, of being diffusive. "The Church, that lives through time, is missionary by her very nature," the council's *Decree on the Missionary Activity of the Church* (ad Gentes Ch. 1, par. 2) proclaims.

That which gives to the recent council a characteristic note, as you know, is the acknowledgement of the vocation—extended to all the faithful—of the obligation, in fact, which is theirs to "spread and defend the faith both by word and by deed as true witnesses of Christ" (Dogmatic Constitution on the Church, n. 11).

Such acknowledgement is specified in the statement which extends to all the Catholic laity the right and duty of the apostolic (ib 33; Decree on the Apostolate of the Laity, 2, 3, etc.).

This wonderful and, in a certain sense, new doctrine indicates what the Church does: she calls mankind; she instructs, strengthens, mobilizes men, makes them participants in her salvific mission, awakens in them the conscience of a mutual Messianism and promotes in each of them a devotion to the cause of Christ, not because of a dream of conquest and power, but because of a pledge of love for all the living and for the glory of God's kingdom.

We would like at this point to ask each of you whether you have given attention to this new apostolic vitality which must now permeate the spirit of those who call themselves Catholics, and which must enable all of them to give a new and positive testimony of Christ. This should be the "post-council." This should be the renewal, the *aggiornamento* augured by the ecumenical council.

In this respect you will observe two different and divergent phenomena. That of the sons of the Church who would call themselves tired of being Catholics and who take advantage of this period of revision and settlement in the practical life of the Church to debate everything, to set up a systematic and contradictory criticism of ecclesiastical discipline; to seek an easier path to Christianity—a Christianity without the invigorating aid of experience and of the development of its tradition; a Christianity conforming with the spirit of the opinion of others and with the customs of the world; a Christianity which is noncommital, non-dogmatic, non-"clerical," as they say.

How can such a weariness of being Catholic logically derive from the council?

The other phenomenon is, instead, the discovery of the joy of being Catholic and together with joy, the new operative vigor which inspires many hearts with desires, hopes, aims, daring to accomplish a new apostolic activity.

The council raised up a generation of vigilant spirits who have heard the voice of the Church calling and imploring them to a greater apostolic effort; a generation that has set itself free from following the crowd, from passiveness, from acquiescence, which reduces so many in our modern world to spiritual slavery. A generation that has imposed on itself some sacrifices—great sacrifices in some cases—in order to be available for performing the good works of the Church. Some have not been afraid to offer their lives to Christ (the phenomenon of adult vocations is significant and magnificent). Others, laity as well—at times husbands and wives—have left for mission countries. Others still, remaining at their place of work, have decided on a profound spiritual renewal and a more generous and Church-centered activity. They have "chosen sanctity" and sanctity implies the charity of the apostolate.

Sons and daughters, who are listening to us: Are you among these?

We hope so, we wish so, with our apostolic blessing.

THE SUFFERING CHURCH

BELOVED SONS AND DAUGHTERS, you know that in this post-council period we reserve this brief conversation for some modest considerations with reference to the Church, trying thus to suggest simple and good thoughts as a remembrance of the weekly general audience.

Well then, last Wednesday, following such a general audience, during which we spoke a few words on the militant Church, we received in another and subsequent audience a group of humble visitors who touched us very deeply. They were blind and deaf-mutes, mercifully assisted and guided by good persons with hearts of gold.

These unfortunate visitors made us think at once: Are not these perhaps also the Church?

The aspect of their most unhappy condition was filled with serenity, a bit concerned at the moment, knowing themselves to be in the presence of the Pope, but also trusting, as though it were a meeting with an old acquaintance, with a father who, they seemed to feel, would have for them, in fact would owe them, a particular preference.

Poor sons! What a pity! What affectionate compassion they stirred in our heart!

At one point there rose from some of them—the blind—a thinly audible sound, a timid song, becoming at once more assured and joyous. Those poor unfortunates were not crying, were not clamoring; they were singing.

Our heart was filled with tenderness and admiration. How we wished that we could comfort, heal those poor creatures, condemned to a perennial sorrowful existence! And there came back to our mind the question: Are not these sufferers perhaps also the Church, the sons of the Church, symbols of the Church, these who are tried by misfortune, who are so sustained by the faith, so aided by charity, so consoled by mercy?

Oh, yes! They and many others like them offer to us the view of the suffering Church, which we might well say is the true Church of the evangelical beatitudes, the true Church of experienced reality, the Church enduring with forebearance in the drama of history, the Church yearning and weeping for the life promised to those who have carried the cross with Christ.

We believe that it is proper and dutiful to reflect on the relationship between the Church of Christ and suffering humanity. The idea of the Church is by its nature associated with that of a fortune, of happiness, of a kingdom full of light and life. Thus we easily forget that the complete happiness which it announces, promises and realizes, is, momentarily—in other words during our earthly life—essentially spiritual and never total.

It is the beatitude of conscience and of hope, which will have its fullness, only after our pilgrimage through time. The beatitudes of the Gospel cast the fulfillment of their promises into the future. For, in fact, as St. Paul says, "in hope were we saved" (Rom. 8:24), and as St. Peter writes: "God . . . has begotten us again . . . into a living hope" (1 Peter 1:3).

This means that the Church, that is to say the Christian religion, is not an insurance company against the ills of the present life. Indeed, if we observe carefully, we will see that it is a society in which human sufferings find a preferential welcome.

The Church is indeed entirely dedicated to relieving the sufferings of men—particularly sin, sorrow, misery, and death. It is compassionate toward every human shortcoming and this is precisely why there is a profound understanding between the Church and the man who suffers. In principle, and often in actual practice, no philanthropy can compete with charity in solicitude for the needs of man. Charity adds to all natural motives a supernatural assessment of the dignity of each human being, recognized as a son of God and a brother of Christ. In addition it brings home the urgency of the supreme evangelical precept —that of loving those who are weaker, more lonely, more needy and more stricken with suffering.

Those who know how to evaluate well this relationship, can understand the tendency of the Church to bend lovingly to the poor and the unhappy; in fact, to make of them her predilected children, and to give to herself the humble and glorious title of the Church of the Poor, and furthermore to propose poverty to herself, as a program.

The first beatitude of the sermon on the mount always resounds in the heart of the Church. We heard its echo becoming increasingly stronger and winning during the council (cf. Decree on the Pastoral Office of Bishops, n. 13; and Decree on the Ministry and Life of Priests, n. 6).

Whoever considers attentively this relationship between the Church and human suffering will also be able, too, to understand something of the mystery of adversity which the Church herself encounters and suffers. The Passion of the Lord, the head of the Church, continues in His members, in His Mystical Body, the Church (cf. Col. 1:24).

As you know this is the history of the Church, not only in the past but in the present in not a few regions of the world. According to the council: "Just as Christ carried out the work of redemption in poverty and oppression, so the Church is called on to follow the same path so that it might communicate the fruits of salvation to men" (Constitution on the Church, n. 8).

St. Augustine says the Church "continues her pilgrimage amidst the persecutions of the world and God's consolations" (De civ. Dei, 18, 51, 2; PL 41, 614).

Yes, beloved children, we must realize that we belong not to a triumphant Church but to a militant Church, contested and suffering.

Will we want to love the Church less, because of this? Will we not want to take part in her poverty and passion?

Will we forget that the Church, also in her suffering, and precisely because of such suffering, experiences at once the consolations of God and "overflows with joy in all" her "troubles" (2 Cor. 7:4)?

Will we not perhaps love our Mother, holy Church, the more precisely because she is suffering?

This is the invitation we extend to all of you, together with our apostolic blessing.

THE HUMBLE, PENITENT CHURCH

BELOVED SONS AND DAUGHTERS, seeing ourselves surrounded as at this moment by many unknown faces, thinking that many of the persons present meet us for the first time and know of this central See of the Church only the picture of this audience; and recalling how easy it is for a transient visitor, a hurried tourist or a hasty observer to judge by curious and often insignificant details the entire ecclesiastical world, its mission, its morality and its religion, a doubt arises in our heart as to the good, edifying and happy nature of the impression which this meeting will leave in the hearts of our visitors.

What image, what concept of the Church and of the Pope will they remember about this moment?

What judgment, what attitude, spiritual or practical, will they have regarding Catholic Rome?

If afterward we think that the historical visage, the human aspect and the external face of the Roman Church show evidence of many defects, inconsistencies and weaknesses, we then ask ourselves: Will esteem and empathy toward the Church herself have increased or, on the contrary, lessened in these persons? Will their faith have been strengthened or, on the contrary, shaken?

And if we think of the many criticisms, suspicions and prejudices which the modern mentality—not excluding, often, that of the good and the wise—has in regard to our apostolic office and to the Church, we ask ourselves if the welcome, so simple and brief, which we extend to those who come here may not be more apt to arouse in them feelings of disfavor and of weariness than feelings of empathy and assent.

True, beloved children, that the acclamations and signs of affection and devotion with which you greet us assure us of the goodness of your intentions and of the faithfulness of your hearts.

Nevertheless, we do not want to omit discussing for a moment the supposition that your impression of this audience and, generally, of the experience which you may have of the life of the Church might be negative. Could it not happen to everyone to have unhappy impressions of the Church?

What, therefore, shall we say to you? In some previous audiences we reviewed the glorious names that characterize the Church: the Kingdom of God and the City of God, the House of God, Fold and Flock of Christ, Spouse of Christ, and so forth.

We likewise named some of the aspects under which the activity of the Church is presented: a praying Church, a missionary and militant Church, a poor and suffering Church, and so forth.

We will now say to you that there is another aspect of the Church in this world, that of the humble Church, of the Church that knows her human limitations, her own failings, her own need of God's mercy and the forgiveness of men.

Yes, this is also a penitent Church, one who preaches and practices penitence; one who does not hide her own failings but deplores them; one who willingly identifies herself with a sinning humanity in order that from a consciousness of a common misery the Church might draw a deeper sorrow for sin, a more urgent plea for divine mercy and a more humble trust in the salvation for which men hope.

The Church is humble not only in the rank and file of the faithful, but also and above all in the highest ranks of the hierarchy, which in the realization and exercise of her life-giving and moderating powers on behalf of the people of God knows that she must use them for the edification and service of souls. This is true at the highest level, that of Peter, who defines himself as the "Servant of God" and who feels more than anyone else the disproportion between the mission he has received from Christ and his own weakness and unworthiness, always recalling the exclamation of the Apostle fisherman: "Depart from me, Lord, for I am a sinner" (Luke 5:8).

And here we have a singular and stupendous fact, the fact of the holiness and indefectibility of the Church and of Christ's representation in it, even when churchmen are personally deficient. The Church of Peter enjoys an assistance from Christ and a presence of the Holy Spirit which makes it impossible for the powers of evil to prevail (cf. Matt. 16:18). Indeed the Church in her entirety does not cease to be loved by Christ even in the most perilous moments of her human fragility, nor does she lose at those times her instrumental holiness in the exercise of her pastoral functions, but remains always capable of producing sanctity and salvation "for the building up of the Body of Christ" (Eph. 4:12).

This observation, which would take us to the delicate study of God's action in His Church, authorizes us to make to you, beloved sons and daughters, a twofold recommendation:

Endeavor to know the Church well, to know her better. This is the first recommendation.

Do not be satisfied with superficial impressions, do not judge the Church only by her human face and the external garments she wears. Come to know her in the variety, richness and profundity of her many aspects, in the human-divine mystery of her interior being, and in the holiness and necessity of her mission of salvation.

And, in the second place, though you may even come across deficiences and evils in the Church, do not allow them to extinguish, but rather to enkindle your love for the Church even more.

We will repeat the words of Jesus: "Blessed is he who is not scandalized in me" (Matt. 11:6), but who instead gives ever greater fidelity, testimony and service to the Church the greater are the needs which she manifests.

SOURCES OF THE CHURCH'S VITALITY

BELOVED SONS AND DAUGHTERS, the Church lives, we were saying. But at once a spontaneous question arises: On what does the Church live? What is the secret of her vitality? The question is spontaneous and legitimate. Perhaps you posed such a question to yourselves: From what does the Church draw her energy, her subsistence?

From what does the Church draw her ability to last throughout time; to spread herself, in the world; in fact, to grow, to renew herself, to rejuvenate herself? This is a spontaneous and legitimate question, though an extremely difficult one. To observe a living being is easy for everyone, but to guess the principles of its life is a very arduous thing, and in great part above our power of knowing. It is so in reference to the Church. She is like a blossoming tree. But what are the roots that make her own springtime always flourishing and new?

Beloved children, we purposely propose to you a similar curiosity. Try to respond to it. Our exhortation is one which must mark your memory of this audience. And if you try to give some answer, you will find that it will not be an easy one.

We do not claim at all, in a conversation so brief and informal as this, to expound organically the doctrine which gives some reason for the vitality of the Church.

It is sufficient for us to present to you some starting point as a stimulus for better research.

For example, is temporal prosperity the reason for the well-being of the Church? Is it riches? Today, anyone wishing to attain an authentic concept of the Church at once answers no; he finds, in fact, that abundance of economic means is in many cases more damaging than propitious to the Church. The pages of history document this fact; the words of the Gospel proclaim it.

Temporal means are indeed necessary for the life of the Church, but only insofar as they furnish bread for her life and are always rigorously kept within the bounds of the purpose of her spiritual mission.

And fortunately it can be said that this is now the mentality and practice of the men of the Church. We thank God. And we credit this disinterested attitude toward economic matters, this poverty which the Lord has taught us, for the discovery that such an attitude is not indeed an impediment to the true prosperity of the Church but a source of spiritual strength, of freedom, wisdom and courage.

We could similarly speak in regard to temporal power: It is not from this that the Church draws her vital energies.

Likewise we could, in a way, say also in regard to profane culture: "That our faith," St. Paul writes, "might rest not on the wisdom of men, but on the power of God" (1 Cor. 2:4-5).

And then? And then we must dare go beyond the threshold of the Gospel and study the principles from which the Lord wishes to draw the fruitfulness of the spiritual and social institution which is the Church founded by Him.

We shall now dwell only upon moral principles, in fact upon only one of them, though one fundamental to the system of the Christian religion. We at once encounter the well known paradox: Christ based the moral life of His followers on a basis which we would call negative: renunciation, abnegation, sacrifice and the Cross.

All of us remember His tremendous words: "For he who would save his life will lose it; but he who loses his life for my sake . . . will save it" (Mark 8:35; John 12:24).

If any of us believed that the life of the Church could be renewed by suppressing the mortifications and vexations, small or large, which pertain to her by reason of moral requirements, or of an acknowledged ascetic custom, he would not properly interpret the fundamental law of the Gospel spirit from which precisely the Church receives her vitality.

This vitality does not derive from the search for a well-being greedy for convenience and appearance, fed by hedonism and egotism, which often characterize the comfortable, frivolous and pleasure-loving practice of the modern world. It derives such growth rather from a silent and constant practice of the virtues that together mortify and fortify the student of Christ: from patient suffering, from faithful obedience, from an austere simplicity, from the imitation of Christ, of a crucified Christ (cf. 1 Cor. 1:23).

We are not preaching here, nor are we prolonging this reflection. We wish, however, to mention certain episodes among the many that we learn of so as to document this thought of ours.

The first episode we read in L'OSSERVATORE ROMANO. A group of university students in Padua gave up their vacations in order to build a house for two large poverty-stricken families in a village in the Paduan countryside who were obliged to live in inadequate and uncomfortable dwellings. Is this not a beautiful example of Christian vitality

The second episode is given to us once more by L'OSSERVATORE ROMANO: "News has been received in Rome that about two months ago the Chinese priest, Kiam Lau Mai-Chung of the Swatow diocese, died in a forced-labor camp of Kiangsi in continental China.

"Born in 1915, he had been ordained in 1944. Arrested in 1955, he was imprisoned in a forced-labor camp, where he died after 11 years of sufferings, borne in a Christian manner."

This could appear as a sign of death rather than one of life of the Church. But will not precisely these sufferings and this martyrdom be the seed for a future revival of Catholicism in that immense country, always so dear to us?

The third episode has been referred to us by a traveler returning from a visit to the by now famous leprosarium of Father Damian on the island of Molokai in the Pacific ocean.

He relates that because of a privilege reserved to priests, he was able to go near the section of the most deformed and repellent lepers. There he approached a humble, most unfortunate creature, horribly eaten away by leprosy, which had devoured her eyes, transforming them into two bleeding and frightening cavities, and which has demolished her extremities, both hands and feet, confining her for years in immobility and suffering as great as a system still surviving under such painful conditions can bear.

Well, the poor, patient, leper woman, having been told that she was speaking with a priest en route to Rome, had the simple and sublime daring to whisper this wonderful confession: I am glad for my state, because I have thus been able to know Jesus Christ and to be Catholic.

She then said she was happy to send to the Pope her devout and filial greeting, together with the offering of the merit of her sufferings.

What do you say to this? We believe these to be the powers that make the Church alive and holy and which confer on her the glory of reflecting Jesus Christ. Her perennial vitality springs from these sources. This is because in God's kingdom (as, after all, also in the natural order) only love is fruitful; and love sums up its highest expression in the giving of self, in sacrifice.

May our apostolic blessing aid you, beloved children, to understand, to meditate, to live the mystery of sacrifice, of the Christian law of dying in order to live, and of the generous and heroic love with which the living and immortal Church nourishes herself.

THE CHURCH, SIGN OF SALVATION

BELOVED SONS AND DAUGHTERS, think with us for a moment. The great question which the council has posed to the conscience of God's people (who, in their full and perfect significance are none other than the Church, one, holy, catholic and apostolic), and has also posed to the world for its consideration, is that of the relationship between Christ and the Church.

This relationship may be sought and defined in different ways. The Church, for example, has been said to be the institution founded by Christ, as He Himself said: "I will build my Church" (Matt. 16:18); a living foundation, however, so much so that the council calls her "the visible structure through which He communicates truth and grace to all" (Constitution on the Church, n. 8); therefore the continuation of Christ throughout history, the extension, the repetition, by analogy, of the mystery of the Incarnate Word (ibid.): the Mystical Body of Christ.

The Church, therefore, is the channel and boundary, under different aspects, of the salvific divine action in humanity. She is the communication, sign and presence of Christ.

Between Christ and the Church there exists a manifest relationship which prompts us to think of a marriage, of a mystical identity. This is why the Church has been mentioned by the ecumenical council itself "as the universal sacrament of salvation" (Constitution on the Church, n. 48) and as "a sacrament of unity" (ibid., n. 1 and 9).

Sacrament means sign. A sign is something which conceals and at the same time uncovers and reveals a reality. A reality not at once known but indicated, manifested by the sign: signified.

If the Church is a sacrament, in other words, a sacred sign, it may be very interesting to explore this sign, to seek Christ "signified" in the Church.

The search may be carried out in different ways, as we also said before. Today we indicate one of the most direct ways, taught to us by the Lord Himself.

He said: "By this will all men know that you are my disciples, if you have love for one another" (John 13:35).

For us this is one of the strongest and most profound statements of Our Lord. It is His testament, His most profound desire, that for which He has chosen to remain and live still in temporal history after His ascension beyond the limits of time to the Father.

Charity—the agape, the dilectio (love-feast and love)—among the followers of the Lord, profound beyond limits and extending in all directions as was His own charity, is the great and new precept of Christian teaching. When it is realized in practice, there we will find fidelity to the Master. And if indeed our charity tends to imitate (we could never say equal!) that limitless and divine charity of Jesus, then Jesus is represented—Jesus is present. Our charity becomes a sign of Christ.

Beloved children! Do we behold similar signs of Christ? Do we have in the Church charitable facts that make us perceive His presence among us? Is the Church still today validated by charity in her possession of Christ? The charity founded on love of God, the charity that solves all conflicts of human coexistence, the charity which is given without limit and without reward?

Yes, yes, beloved children of this holy Catholic Church; all the Church is resplendent with such signs and such evidence! Open your eyes and see how many lights of that charity radiate from her mantle, from her historical and concrete garment, we mean to say, a garment not at all equally splendid and new, an ancient garment and so human which is always in need of being repaired and renewed (as the council attempted to do), but all of it covered with sparkling gems of that presence of Christ which true charity evokes again in our midst.

See how many men and women still today accept the vocation of immolating their young and budding lives in the practice and evidence of charity!

See how many humble priests give their lives as pastors, chaplains, teachers to inspire charity in God's people! See how many bishops do their utmost to promote this charity, to work in its service, to embody it in their own lives and to sacrifice themselves for it!

Amidst so much distress and sadness, we have this daily, superlative comfort of seeing each day sparkling examples of heroic charity in holy Church; we could make a journal of charity, which would be the daily document of the moving and wonderful signs of Christ's actual presence among us.

Fortunately these signs are everywhere: in our welfare organizations, our institutions for the care of the sick, in our schools, in our Christian character formation of children and youth toward good works, and in the missions. And if the spirit of charity truly prompts these manifold activities, then Christ appears through them because they are an evidence of Christianity in action.

Even if their religious intention were not manifest but the goodness of the action is clear, as we see during these days when assistance is being given to populations stricken by terrible floods, do we not perceive in these generous sentiments and the brotherly impulse of such solidarity a distinguishing mark, a certain humanity which tells us at least in these most noble manifestations that our civilization is still Christian? The "signs" show it.

To us believers similar acts of generosity and charity hold the particular good that all of us can carry out with that spirit that transforms them; all of us have a certain capacity to make of our Church—to which we are fortunate to belong—a sign, a sign of Christ; to thus make Christ present in our generation and own locality.

The council says this: "For the spirit of poverty and of charity are the glory and authentication of the

Church of Christ" (Church in the Modern World, n. 88).

To you, beloved children, we extend, together with our blessing, the invitation to multiply these signs of superhuman value: the soul that fulfills them will benefit from them; the brethren that receive them will benefit therefrom; the world that admires them will benefit; the Church that therein finds herself happily of Christ, will likewise benefit.

BUILDING THE CHURCH WITH CHRIST

Beloved sons and daughters, we invite you to consider the word of God which seems to resound everlastingly in this basilica and which—in looking at the circular band of the large-lettered inscriptions that decorate the basilica, up above, in solemn and eloquent mosaics—you can read, as though it had been pronounced to be proclaimed here: "I will build my Church" (Matt. 16:18). "I will build," have you ever probed into the meaning of these words?

Here is a prophetic statement. It has Christ as its subject and it refers to the future; it has the Church as its object, depicted as a building in the process of construction. Christ is the architect of the building and indeed the workman: I will build. You know that this image of the Church-edifice is among the more frequent and more expressive of the images. St. Paul makes use of it (1 Cor. 3:9; Eph. 2:20-22). St. Peter explains it (1 Pet. 2:5). Both develop its concept in relation to the material of construction; a material which is formed by the faithful themselves, "living rock," where there can only ensue a living edifice, "a spiritual house," a harmonious and unitary sum-total, a visible, organic and social order, a sacred humanity, where God lives.

This is the "house of God" (cf. Gen. 28:17); which the letter to the Hebrews will show even more clearly to be nothing other than us, the followers of Christ; "we are the house of Christ" (Heb. 3:3-6).

You know also that this symbolic image of the edifice which refers to the Church is among those recalled by the council (Constitution on the Church, n.6) in the constitution relative to the Church itself. It is, furthermore, the image most frequently used in common language to call a material edifice a church, but where the Church, the assembly of faithful, gathers and expresses itself as a spiritual edifice.

However we do not now wish to speak to you of this aspect of the symbol. We wish to invite you to reflect on the expressive power of the term used by Christ: "I will build."

The statement indicates permanent action on the part of the Lord in regard to His Church. It indicates the dynamic character which the life of the Church, depicted as a building under construction, assumes. It indicates a continual development which is foreordained for it by the very concept of the work—which must be accomplished according to a concrete, visible, well-planned design of which Christ is the architect and not left to the judgment of capricious workmen. The Church must be constructed. She is always an incomplete building which prolongs in temporary history her determined plan of accomplishment.

If we recall that Christ's action after His ascension is, by His divine mandate, fulfilled by the Church herself, by those who in the Church have the function of promoting the continuance of Jesus' work, this perfective concept of the Church becomes very instructive for us. It becomes a program if we think that all of us are called to collaborate in the mystical and positive construction of the Church.

It seems to us proper to recall this fundamental principle of the ecclesiastical life to better conform our minds to the directive lines which are to guide our thought and action in this post-council period. We must build the Church with Christ and for Christ.

Everyone knows that the council has set the Church in motion in every aspect of her life, thus giving all of us the awareness of a renewal, of a new labor to undertake, a development to be realized. It is an awareness which fills our hearts with fervor and hope, but not without a certain amount of anxiety, for the right orientation and happy outcome of this renewal.

Let us say first of all that we cannot share the diffidence and discomfort of those who are placing obstacles in the way of such a renewal, as if it went against the stability of the ecclesiastical order, as if fidelity to tradition involved immobility and inertia and as if the temporal Church had already arrived at her complete and definitive expression. The words of Christ on the contrary are prophetic words: "I will build." The work awaits its continuation. Today all of us must be workers in the Church, that is, active members, apostles and missionaries, not indifferent spectators, not fussy and lazy critics.

But on the other hand, we cannot give in to the temptation of believing that innovations derived from the doctrines and decrees of the council give the go-ahead for any kind of arbitrary change or justify frivolous and irresponsible undertakings out of keeping with the design which must be followed in building. We must be profoundly convinced that we cannot demolish the Church of yesterday to construct a new one today.

We cannot forget or call into question, what the Church has been teaching as authoritative until now in order to substitute personal and arbitrary theories and new concepts for secure doctrine. We cannot borrow from the current, changing and secular opinions of our time a criterion for the thought and action of the Church community as if such opinions were the "consensus of the faithful," or witnesses to Christian truth which the faithful, guided by the teaching authority (magisterium) of the Church, have the ability and the obligation to profess.

We cannot solve difficult questions or weaken exacting laws by adapting changes based on history and subjective interpretations, discarding as ancient and obsolete the dogmatic canons, that is to say, the clear, stable and authoritative canons of the Church's teaching, and evading the unchanging demands of the word of God and of its strict traditional expression.

We must instead continue the construction of the Church by conforming her new additions to the design pre-established by Christ and by building with trust and loyalty on the structure already in existence.

It is this positive psychology which must guide the constructive work of the Church in the aftermath of the Second Vatican Council.

We are happy to note its full development in many occurrences of the present life of the Church. The work of the bishops' conferences, for example, introduces and inaugurates a new and fruitful period of the history of the Church.

The spontaneous action of the laity, coordinated with the directive plans of the responsible hierarchy, is a very comforting and promising fact.

Charitable activity, which is reawakened everywhere, is already a fact worthy of praise and encouragement. How happy we are in seeing the youth in the vanguard of such activity!

To build, to edify Catholic life, with courage, order and patience. May this be also for you the commitment which our apostolic blessing gives to you.

THE CHURCH, CHAMPION OF SOCIAL JUSTICE AND PROGRESS

GREETINGS TO YOU WORKERS, an affectionate welcome to you who represent your brothers in faith and work throughout the world. Be assured that you are received here as dear and faithful sons, as workers indeed worthy of carrying the badges of your toil and the expression of your hopes to the Pope, the visible vicar of the Redeemer of the world, your Divine Colleague, the Son of the carpenter, our Lord Jesus Christ!

Why did you come in such large numbers from so many different countries? Because you have a good memory, a memory lasting through several generations and recalling the 75th anniversary of the great words pronounced here. They were the masterly, guiding, liberating words of our predecessor of immortal greatness, Leo XIII, regarding your lot, regarding the "question of the workers" as it was then called. It was the social question rising from the new ideologies and the new methods of industrial production and modern economy.

You remember those words and indeed you assess their importance so well that with the passing years you feel they are stronger and more your own, truly decisive and providing an orientation. And you willingly recognize that they have been a wonderful source of thought and action. It is a source which has generated a tradition of doctrine not only in the world but here, in this very place, giving rise to a series of pontifical documents of utmost value such as the encyclical of Pius XI, *Quadragesimo Anno,* the social messages of Pope Pius XII and the encyclical, *Mater et Magistra,* of Pope John XXIII.

You understand very well that in order to walk forward it is necessary to have light, that to promote social progress it is necessary to have a doctrine, an ideology as it is called nowadays. It is thought which guides life and if thought reflects truth—the truth about man, the world, history and temporal things—then you can walk forward with assurance and speed. If not your steps become either slow or uncertain or else heavy and wandering.

You understand that here, from this school which is the Catholic Church, from this chair which is the pontifical teaching authority, comes the truth which serves and saves man. Here the teacher of mankind, Christ the Lord, makes us first into disciples and then into secure and free men capable of traversing the roads of true progress.

Your coming therefore assumes in our eyes a twofold significance. It is an act of gratitude and a tacit question. You come to thank that pope of long ago who remains in our memory and to whom we owe so much, and you profess faith and conviction, commitment and hope in those words of his. From here, whence they went forth, you tell him that those words

—the *Rerum Novarum*—were true and good and are still alive and active. Time did not exhaust but tested them, so much so that you still feel them so topical and fruitful as to draw from them the courage for those new developments of the social order with which the world of labor is concerned.

For this act of gratitude and trust, worthy of intelligent men and of faithful sons, we thank you, beloved workers.

And then we seem to perceive in your deepest thoughts a discreet question, almost a need to verify the echo those words of 75 years ago have today in this See. Do they still resound? Do they still have the same accent of authority, of prophecy and of friendship?

Yes, beloved workers, if you listen carefully—that is to say if you pay attention to what the Church teaches and does for your cause today—you will realize that the echo is faithful and indeed has become a more explicit voice, more varied in its motivation and application.

Everything has been said and written in this respect. This very celebration has prompted and will continue to prompt authoritative testimonies of all kinds regarding the endurance and development of pontifical teaching deriving from the Leonine pontificate.

Not only did a literature spring from it which continues to produce pages worthy of consideration and widespread reading, but a body of doctrine has been formed concerning economy, sociology, law, ethics and history—in a word, a whole culture worthy of the name of Christian social teaching.

If by way of example and as a memory of this significant hour we were to reduce the lasting message of this famous encyclical to a few elementary propositions, we could proclaim among others these simple but fundamental axioms:

First: The Church has been thoroughly interested in the social question. Nobody can reproach her for absence from problems, for timidity, superficiality or inconsistency. The Church has heard the "cry of anguish" of the workers' proletariat and even made it her own, not as tinder for hatred and revenge but as a demand for love and justice. Even before concerning herself with the needs and rights of others she frankly recognized her own new duty which the history of human vissitudes placed before, the duty to concern herself with the working world, to place herself at the side of the defenseless and to seek with them and for them better living conditions.

Second: The Church has proclaimed the dignity of labor of whatever kind, so long as it is honest, and supported it with wonderful argumentation. There has been even talk of a "theology of labor" since in the thought of the Church human activity, including that which is manual and executive, has been recognized in its most human and most mysterious implications.

What has the Church not said, what has she not proclaimed regarding the worker, his person, his singularity and his numerical entity in the midst of the crowd (which the Church does not call a "mass" but a "people")? What has the Church left unsaid about his conscience, his liberty, his inalienable and sacrosanct right to bread, to a family, to education, to spiritual hope and profession of religious beliefs?

You workers who are listening now—who more than the Church has esteemed, respected, cared for and loved you as persons?

Third axiom: The Church has made her own the principle of the progress of social justice, that is to say of the necessity of promoting and implementing the common good, not only by its speculative doctrine (which it has maintained ever since the evangelical message proclaiming blessed all who hunger and thirst after justice) but also in its practical teaching. This promotion of the common good involves reforming existing legal norms whenever they do not take into sufficient account the just distribution of the advantages and burdens of life in society.

Fourth axiom: The Church has never been afraid to descend from the religious sphere proper to her to the sphere of the concrete conditions of social life. Like the Samaritan in the Gospel's parable, the Church has descended from her mount, that is to say from the purely religious concern with the cult of worship, and become a minister of charity—not only individual but social charity. She has shown her concern in the economic field. She has spoken on the relationship between capital and labor. She has pronounced on the labor contract, on wages, assistance, family allowances, private property, savings—on a hundred practical questions essentially connected with the honest and legitimate necessities of life.

Her charity armed herself with progressive demands which she described as human and Christian and therefore right. She assessed the aspirations and interests of the poorer classes and did not hesitate to search among them with wisdom and prudence and a far-reaching courage to find new rights to be satisfied. She aspired and still aspires to obtain legislation contrary to privilege and selfishness, which will protect the weak, the humble and the disinherited. Indeed she has demanded that the state intervene, not in order to take over the rights and functions which belong in a free society to citizens, whether individual or associated, but to protect the freedom and the equality of the citizens themselves and to assume the exercise of those activities which only public authority can pursue if the common good is to be completely guaranteed.

Fifth axiom: The Church has recognized the right to form trade unions. She has defended and promoted this right, overcoming a certain theoretical and historical preference for corporative forms and mixed associations. She took cognizance not only of the strength of numbers which the fact of unionizing was bound to exert upon a society oriented toward democracy, but also the fruitfulness of the new order which could spring from workers' unions—an awareness on the part of the worker of his dignity and his position in the social framework, a sense of discipline and solidarity, a spur to professional and cultural advancement, a capacity to participate in the productive cycle no longer as a mere executive instrument, but to some extent at least as a sharer in responsibility and an interested participant.

There is then a sixth axiom, the most discussed and the most difficult of all of them. The Church has not and cannot adhere to social, ideological and political movements which, in finding their origins and strength in Marxism, have maintained its negative principles and the methods resulting from the incomplete and therefore false conception of man, of history and of the world which is typical of radical Marxism.

The atheism which it professes and promotes is not in favor of the scientific concept of the cosmos and of civilization, but is a blindness which man and society will have to pay for in the end with the gravest consequences. The materialism which derives from it exposes man to experience and temptations which are extremely harmful. It extinguishes his true spirituality and his transcendent hope.

Class struggle raised to a system harms and impedes social peace and inevitably ends in violence and oppression, leading to the abolition of liberty and the establishment of a ponderously authoritarian system naturally inclined toward totalitarianism.

The Church does not bypass any claims for justice and progress of the workers. Let it be once more affirmed that the Church by rectifying these errors and deviations does not exclude from her love any man, any worker.

All these things are well known, the more so because of a historical experience now in progress which does not permit illusions. But they are painful things, too, because they exert an ideological and practical pressure on the world of labor. They purport to be interpreting the aspirations and promoting the claims of labor, thus giving rise to great difficulties and great divisions. We shall not discuss them now except to recall that those same words to which you, Christian workers, are now giving a testimony of honor and gratitude are the same which admonish us against placing our trust in erroneous and dangerous ideologies and invite us rather to another consideration with which we shall conclude these summary observations.

And let this be our seventh axiom, as is proclaimed by the encyclical, *Rerum Novarum,* and those which followed. It is the indispensable role the Church has in the promotion of social progress and in the solution of the well-known and recurrent social question. It is not a purely instrumental role but, we should say, a transfiguring one, owing to the principles, the energies, the consolations, the hopes which religion—we mean the real one, the one which is fortunately ours, the Christian one—instills into the entire world of labor. Christ, as you know, calls forth an experience of Himself, of life, of society, of temporary things, of time itself, of justice and love which has no parallel and for which there is no definition except that of the beatitude He proclaimed to the poor, to the sorrowful, to the persecuted, to the righteous, to those who hunger for justice and love.

Well then, Christian workers, we entrust you to Christ. To Christ—we exhort you—as to the light of your individual conscience, as to the center of the movement of Christian workers, to which you desire today to give worldwide dimensions; to the institution of which we are happy and proud to salute and to which we give our fatherly and trusting encouragement. In order that you should not lack the conviction that Christ awaits you, that Christ welcomes you, that Christ unites you, that Christ strengthens and sanctifies you, may there descend upon you from His humble vicar the apostolic blessing.

The Thought of Vatican II on the Church

THE THOUGHT OF VATICAN II ON THE CHURCH

In the old Testament the revelation of the Kingdom is often conveyed by means of metaphors. In the same way the inner nature of the Church is now made known to us in different images taken either from tending sheep or cultivating the land, from building or even from family life and betrothals.

The Church is a *sheepfold* whose one and indispensable door is Christ (Jn. 10:1-10). It is a flock of which God Himself foretold He would be the shepherd (cf. Is. 40:11; Ez. 34:11 ff.), and whose sheep, although ruled by human shepherds, are nevertheless continuously led and nourished by Christ Himself, the Good Shepherd and the Prince of the shepherds (cf. Jn. 10, 11; 1 Pet. 5, 4), who gave His life for the sheep (cf. John 10:11-16).

The Church is a piece of land to be cultivated, the tillage of God (1 Cor. 3:9). On that land the ancient olive tree grows whose holy roots were the Prophets and in which the reconciliation of Jews and Gentiles has been brought about and will be brought about (Rom. 11:13-26). That land, like a choice vineyard, has been planted by the heavenly Husbandman (Matt.

21:33-43; cf. Is. 5:1 ff.). The true vine is Christ who gives life and the power to bear abundant fruit to the branches, that is, to us, who through the Church re-John 10, 11; 1 Pet. 5, 4), who gave His life for the sheep (cf. John 10:11-16).

Often the Church has also been called the *building* of God (1 Cor. 3:9). The Lord Himself compared Himself to the stone which the builders rejected, but which was made into the cornerstone (Matt. 21:42; cf. Acts 4:11; 1 Pet. 2:7; Ps. 117:22). On this foundation the Church is built by the apostles (cf. 1 Cor. 3:11), and from it the Church receives durability and consolidation. This edifice has many names to describe it: the house of God (1 Tim. 3:15) in which dwells His *family*; the household of God in the Spirit (Eph. 2:19-22); the dwelling place of God among men (Apoc. 21:3); and, especially, the holy *temple*. This Temple, symbolized in places of worship built out of stone, is praised by the Holy Fathers and, not without reason, is compared in the liturgy to the Holy City, the New Jerusalem (cf. Oirgenes, *In Mt.* 16:21: PG 13, 1443 C; Tertullianus, *Adv Marc.* 3,7: PL 2, 357 C; CSEL 47, 3 p. 386). As living stones we here on earth are built into it (1 Pet. 2:5). John contemplates this holy city coming down from heaven at the renewal of the world as a bride made ready and adorned for her husband (Apoc. 21:1 f.).

The Church, further, "that Jerusalem which is above" is also called "our mother" (Gal. 4:26; cf. Apoc. 12:17). It is described as the spotless *spouse* of the spotless Lamb (Apoc. 19:7; 21:2, 9; 22:17), whom Christ "loved and for whom He delivered Himself up that He might sanctify her" (Eph. 5:26), whom He unites to Himself by an unbreakable covenant, and whom He unceasingly "nourishes and cherishes" (Eph. 5:29), and whom once purified, He willed to be cleansed and joined to Himself, subject to Him in love and fidelity (cf. Eph. 5:24), and whom, finally, He filled with heavenly gifts for all eternity, in order that we may know the love of God and of Christ for us, a love which surpasses all knowledge (cf. Eph. 3:19). The Church, while on earth it journeys in a foreign land away from the Lord (cf. 2 Cor. 5:6), is like an exile. It seeks and experiences those things which are above, where Christ is seated at the right-hand of God, where the life of the Church is hidden with Christ in God until it appears in glory with its Spouse (cf. Col. 3:1-4).

DOGMATIC CONSTITUTION ON THE CHURCH, n. 6

The eternal Father, by a free and hidden plan of His own wisdom and goodness, created the whole world. His plan was to raise men to a participation of the divine life. Fallen in Adam, God the Father did not leave men to themselves, but ceaselessly offered helps to salvation, in view of Christ, the Redeemer "who is the image of the invisible God, the firstborn of every creature" (Col. 1:15). All the elect, before time began, the Father "foreknew and predestined to become conformed to the image of His Son, that he should be the firstborn among many brethren" (Rom. 8:29). He planned to assemble in the holy Church all those who would believe in Christ. Already from the beginning of the world the foreshadowing of the Church took place. It was prepared in a remarkable way throughout the history of the people of Israel and by means of the Old Covenant (cf. S. Cyrianus, Epist. 64, 4; PL 3, 1017. CSEL (Hartel) III B, p. 720. S. Hilarius Pict. *In Mt.* 23, 6: PL 9, 1047. S. Augustine, *passim.* S. Cyrillus Alex., *Glaph. in Gen.* 2, 10: PG 69, 110A). In the present era of time the Church was constituted and, by the outpouring of the Spirit, was made manifest. At the end of time it will gloriously achieve completion, when, as is read in the Fathers, all the just, from Adam and "from Abel, the just one, to the last of the elect" (cf. S. Gregorius M., *Hom. in Evang.* 19, 1: PL 76, 1154 B. S. Augustine, *Serm,* 341, 9, 11: PL 39, 1499 s. S. Io. Damascenus, *Adv. Iconocl.* 11: PG 96, 1358), will be gathered together with the Father in the universal Church.

DOGMATIC CONSTITUTION ON THE CHURCH, n. 2

As God did not create man for life in isolation, but for the formation of social unity, so also "it has pleased God to make men holy and save them not merely as individuals, without bond or link between them, but by making them into a single people, a people which acknowledges Him in truth and serves Him in holiness." So from the beginning of salvation history He has chosen men not just as individuals but as members of a certain community. Revealing His mind to them, God called these chosen ones "His people" (Ex. 3:7-12), and even made a covenant with them on Sinai (cf. Exodus 24:1-8).

This communitarian character is developed and consummated in the work of Jesus Christ. For the very Word made flesh willed to share in the human fellowship. He was present at the wedding of Cana, visited the house of Zacchaeus, ate with publicans and sinners. He revealed the love of the Father and the sublime vocation of man in terms of the most common of social realities and by making use of the speech and the imagery of plain everyday life. Willingly obeying the laws of His country, He sanctified those human ties, especially family ones, which are the source of social structures. He chose to lead the life proper to an artisan of His time and place.

In His preaching He clearly taught the sons of God to treat one another as brothers. In His prayers He pleaded that all His disciples might be "one." Indeed as the redeemer of all, He offered Himself for all even to the point of death. "Greater love than this no one has, that one lay down his life for his friends" (John 15:13). He commanded His Apostles to preach to all peoples the Gospel's message that the human race was to become the Family of God, in which the fulness of the Law would be love.

As the firstborn of many brethren and by the giving of His Spirit, He founded after His death and resurrection a new brotherly community composed of all those who receive Him in faith and in love. This He did through His Body, which is the Church. There everyone, as members one of the other, would render mutual service according to the different gifts bestowed on each.

This solidarity must be constantly increased until that day on which it will be brought to perfection. Then, saved by grace, men will offer flawless glory to God as a family beloved of God and of Christ their Brother.

PASTORAL CONSTITUTION ON THE CHURCH IN THE MODERN WORLD, n. 32

The mystery of the holy Church is manifest in its very foundation. The Lord Jesus set it on its course by preaching the Good News, that is, the coming of the Kingdom of God, which, for centuries, had been promised in the Scriptures: "The time is fulfilled, and the kingdom of God is at hand" (Mark 1:5; cf. Matt. 4:17). In the word, in the works, and in the presence of Christ, this kingdom was clearly open to the view of men. The Word of the Lord is compared to a seed which is sown in a field (Mark 4:14); those who hear the Word with faith and become part of the little flock of Christ (Luke 12:32), have received the Kingdom itself. Then, by its own power the seed sprouts and grows until harvest time (cf. Mark 4:26-29). The Miracles of Jesus also confirm that the Kingdom has already arrived on earth: "If I cast out devils by the finger of God, then the kingdom of God has come upon you" (Luke 11:20; cf. Matt. 12:28). Before all things, however, the Kingdom is clearly visible in the very Person of Christ, the Son of God and the Son of Man, who came "to serve and to give His life as a ransom for many" (Mark 10:45).

When Jesus, who had suffered the death of the cross for mankind, had risen, He appeared as the one constituted as Lord, Christ and eternal Priest (cf. Acts 2:36; Heb. 5:6; 7:17-21), and He poured out on His disciples the Spirit promised by the Father (cf. Acts 2.33). From this source the Church, equipped with the gifts of its Founder and faithfully guarding His precepts of charity, humility and self-sacrifice, receives the mission to proclaim and to spread among all peoples the Kingdom of Christ and of God and to be, on earth, the initial budding forth of that kingdom. While it slowly grows, the Church strains toward the completed Kingdom and, with all its strength, hopes and desires to be united in glory with its King.

DOGMATIC CONSTITUTION ON THE CHURCH, n. 5

From the very beginning, the Lord Jesus "called to Himself those whom He wished; and He caused twelve of them to be with Him, and to be sent out preaching" (Mark 3:13; cf. Matt. 10:1-42). Thus the Apostles were the first budding-forth of the New Israel, and at the same time the beginning of the sacred hierarchy. Then, when He had by His death and His resurrection completed once for all in Himself the mysteries of our salvation and the renewal of all things, the Lord, having now received all power in heaven and on earth (cf. Matt. 28:18), before He was taken up into heaven (cf. Acts 1:11), founded His Church as the sacrament of salvation and sent His Apostles into all the world just as He Himself had been sent by the Father (cf. John 20:21), commanding them: "Go, therefore, and make disciples of all nations, baptizing them in the name of the Father and of the Son and of the Holy Spirit; teaching them to observe all that I have commanded you" (Matt. 28:19 ff.). "Go into the whole world, preach the Gospel to every creature. He who believes and is baptized shall be saved; but he who does not believe, shall be condemned" (Mark 16:15 ff.). Whence the duty that lies on the Church of spreading the faith and the salvation of Christ, not only in virtue of the express command which was inherited from the Apostles by the order of bishops, assisted by the priests, together with the successor of Peter and supreme shepherd of the Church, but also in virtue of that life which flows from Christ into His members: "From Him the whole body, being closely joined and knit together through every joint of the system, according to the functioning in due measure of each single part, derives its increase to the building up of itself in love" (Eph. 4:16). The mission of the Church, therefore, is fulfilled by that activity which makes her, obeying the command of Christ and influenced by the grace and love of the Holy Spirit, fully present to all men or nations, in order that, by the example of her life and by her preaching, by the sacraments and other means of grace, she may lead them to the faith, the freedom and the peace of Christ; that thus there may lie open before them a firm and free road to full participation in the mystery of Christ.

DECREE ON THE MISSION ACTIVITY
OF THE CHURCH, n. 5

In order to establish this His holy Church everywhere in the world till the end of time, Christ entrusted to the College of the Twelve the task of teaching, ruling and sanctifying (cf. Mt. 28:18-20). Among their number He selected Peter, and after his confession of faith determined that on him He would build His Church. Also to Peter He promised the keys of the kingdom of heaven (cf. Mt. 16:19, in conjunction with Mt. 18:18), and after His profession of love, entrusted all His sheep to him to be confirmed in faith (cf. Lk. 22:32) and shepherded in perfect unity (cf. Jn. 21:15-18). Christ Jesus Himself was forever to remain the chief cornerstone (cf. Eph. 2:20) and shepherd of our souls (cf. 1 Pet. 2:25; I Vatican Council, Sess. IV [1870], the Constitution *Pastor Aeternus*: Coll. Lac. 7, 482 a).

DECREE ON ECUMENISM, n. 2

When the work which the Father gave the Son to do on earth (cf. Jn. 17:4) was accomplished, the Holy Spirit was sent on the day of Pentecost in order that He might continually sanctify the Church, and thus, all those who believe would have access through Christ in one Spirit to the Father (cf. Eph. 2:18). He is the Spirit of Life, a fountain of water springing up to life eternal (cf. Jn. 4:14; 7:38-39). To men, dead in sin, the Father gives life through Him, until, in Christ, He brings to life their mortal bodies (cf. Rom. 8:10-11). The Spirit dwells in the Church and in the hearts of the faithful, as in a temple (cf. 1 Cor. 3:16; 6:19). In them He prays on their behalf and bears witness to the fact that they are adopted sons (cf. Gal. 4:6; Rom. 8: 15-16, 26). The Church, which the Spirit guides in way of all truth (cf. Jn. 16:13) and which He unified in communion and in works of ministry, He both equips and directs with hierarchical and charismatic gifts and adorns with His fruits (cf. Eph. 4:11-12; 1 Cor. 12:4; Gal. 5:22). By the power of the Gospel He makes the Church keep the freshness of youth. Uninterruptedly He renews it and leads it to perfect union with its Spouse (cf. S. Irenaeus, *Adv. Haer.* III, 24, 1: PG 7, 966 B; Harvey 2, 131; ed. Sagnard, *Sources Chr.*, p. 398). The Spirit and the Bride both say to Jesus, the Lord, "Come!" (cf. Apoc. 22:17)

Thus, the Church has been seen as "a people made one with the unity of the Father, the Son, and the Holy Spirit" (S. Cyprianus, *De Orat. Dom.* 23: PL 4, 553; Hartel, III A, p. 285. S. Augustinus, *Serm.* 71, 20, 33: PL 38, 463 s. S. Io. Damascenus, *Adv. Iconocl.* 12: PG 96, 1358 D.).

DOGMATIC CONSTITUTION ON THE CHURCH, n. 4

The apostolic preaching, which is expressed in a special way in the inspired books, was to be preserved by an unending succession of preachers until the end of tiine. Therefore the Apostles, handing on what they themselves had received, warn the faithful to hold fast to the traditions which they have learned either by word of mouth or by letter (see 2 Thess. 2:15), and to fight in defense of the faith handed on once and for all (see Jude 1:3; cf. Second Council of Nicea: Denzinger 303 [602]; Fourth Council of Constance, session X, Canon 1: Denzinger 336 [650-652]). Now what was handed on by the Apostles includes everything which contributes toward the holiness of life and increase in faith of the people of God; and so the Church, in her teaching, life and worship, perpetuates and hands on to all generations all that she herself is, all that she believes.

DOGMATIC CONSTITUTION ON DIVINE REVELATION, n. 8

By reason of the gift and role of divine maternity, by which she is united with her Son, the Redeemer, and with His singular graces and functions, the Blessed Virgin is also intimately united with the Church. As St. Ambrose taught, the Mother of God is a type of the Church in the order of faith, charity and perfect union with Christ (S. Ambrosius, *Expos. Lc.* II, 7: PL 15, 1555). For in the mystery of the Church, which is itself rightly called mother and virgin, the Blessed Virgin stands out in eminent and singular fashion as exemplar both of virgin and mother. By her belief and obedience, not knowing man but overshadowed by the Holy Spirit, as the new Eve she brought forth on earth the very Son of the Father, showing an undefiled faith, not in the word of the ancient serpent, but in that of God's messenger. The Son whom she brought forth is He whom God placed as the first-born among many brethren (cf. Rom. 8:29), namely the faithful, in whose birth and education she cooperates with a maternal love. DOGMATIC CONSTITUTION ON THE CHURCH, n. 63

Although by the power of the Holy Spirit the Church will remain the faithful spouse of her Lord and will never cease to be the sign of salvation on earth, still she is very well aware that among her members, (cf. St. Ambrose, *De virginitate*, Chapter VIII, n. 48: ML 16, 278), both clerical and lay, some have been unfaithful to the Spirit of God during the course of many centuries; in the present age, too, it does not escape the Church how great a distance lies between the message she offers and the human failings of those to whom the Gospel is entrusted. Whatever be the judgment of history on these defects, we ought to be conscious of them, and struggle against them energetically, lest they inflict harm on spread of the Gospel. The Church also realizes that in working out her relationship with the world she always has great need of the ripening which comes with the experience of the centuries. Led by the Holy Spirit, Mother Church unceasingly exhorts her sons "to purify and renew themselves so that the sign of Christ can shine more brightly on the face of the Church."

PASTORAL CONSTITUTION ON THE CHURCH IN THE MODERN WORLD, n. 43

Just as Christ carried out the work of redemption in poverty and persecution, so the Church is called to follow the same route that it might communicate the fruits of salvation to men. Christ Jesus, "though He was by nature God . . . emptied Himself, taking the nature of a slave" (Phil. 2:6-7), and "being rich, became poor" (2 Cor. 8:9) for our sakes. Thus, the Church, although it needs human resources to carry out its mission, is not set up to seek earthly glory, but to proclaim, even by its own example, humility and self-sacrifice. Christ was sent by the Father "to bring good news to the poor, to heal the contrite of heart" (Luke 4:18), "to seek and to save what was lost" (Luke 19:10). Similarly, the Church encompasses with love all who are afflicted with human suffering and in the poor and afflicted sees the image of its poor and suffering Founder. It does all it can to relieve their need and in them it strives to serve Christ. While Christ, holy, innocent and undefiled (Heb. 7:26), knew nothing of sin (2 Cor. 5:21), but came to expiate only the sins of the people (cf. Heb. 2:17), the Church, embracing in its bosom sinners, at the same time holy and always in need of being purified, always follows the way of penance and renewal. The Church, "like a stranger in a foreign land, presses forward amid the persecutions of the world and the consolations of God" (S. Augustine, *Civ. Dei,* XVIII, 51, 2: PL 41, 614), announcing the cross and death of the Lord until He comes (cf. 1 Cor. 11:26). By the power of the risen Lord it is given strength that it might, in patience and in love, overcome its sorrows and its challenges, both within itself and from without, and that it might reveal to the world, faithfully though darkly, the mystery of its Lord until, in the end, it will be manifested in full light.

DOGMATIC CONSTITUTION ON THE CHURCH, n. 8

Christ summons the Church to continual reformation as she sojourns here on earth. The Church is always in need of this, insofar as she is an institution of men here on earth. Thus if, in various times and circumstances, there have been deficiencies in moral conduct or in church discipline, or even in the way that Church teaching has been formulated—to be carefully distinguished from the deposit of faith itself—these can and should be set right at the opportune moment.

DECREE ON ECUMENISM, n. 6

While helping the world and receiving many benefits from it, the Church has a single intention: that God's kingdom may come, and that the salvation of the whole human race may come to pass. For every benefit which the People of God during its earthly pilgrimage can offer to the human family stems from the fact that the Church is "the universal sacrament of salvation," simultaneously manifesting and exercising the mystery of God's love for man.

For God's Word, by whom all things were made, was Himself made flesh so that as perfect man He might save all men and sum up all things in Himself. The Lord is the goal of human history, the focal point of the longings of history and of civilization, the center of the human race, the joy of every heart and the answer to all its yearnings. He it is Whom the Father raised from the dead, lifted on high and stationed at His right hand, making Him judge of the living and the dead. Enlivened and united in His Spirit, we journey toward the consummation of human history, one which fully accords with the counsel of God's love: "To reestablish all things in Christ, both those in the heavens and those on the earth" (Eph. 11:10).

PASTORAL CONSTITUTION ON THE CHURCH IN THE MODERN WORLD, n. 45

Christ, to be sure, gave His Church no proper mission in the political, economic or social order. The purpose which He set before her is a religious one. But out of this religious mission itself come a function, a light and an energy which can serve to structure and consolidate the human community according to the divine law. As a matter of fact, when circumstances of time and place produce the need, she can and indeed should initiate activities on behalf of all men, especially those designed for the needy, such as the works of mercy and similar undertakings.

PASTORAL CONSTITUTION ON THE CHURCH IN THE MODERN WORLD, n. 42

The Church, the kingdom of Christ now present in mystery, grows visibly through the power of God in the world. This inauguration and this growth are both symbolized by the blood and water which flowed from the open side of a crucified Jesus (cf. Jn. 19:34), and are foretold in the words of the Lord referring to His death on the Cross: "And I, if I be lifted up from the earth, will draw all things to myself" (Jn. 12:32). As often as the sacrifice of the cross in which Christ our Passover was sacrificed (1 Cor. 5:7) is celebrated on the altar, the work of our redemption is carried on, and, in the sacrament of the eucharistic bread, the unity of all believers who form one body in Christ (cf. 1 Cor. 10:17) is both expressed and brought about. All men are called to this union with Christ, who is the light of the world, from whom we go forth, through whom we live, and toward whom our whole life strains.

DOGMATIC CONSTITUTION ON THE CHURCH, n. 3

They are fully incorporated in the society of the Church who, possessing the Spirit of Christ, accept her entire system and all the means of salvation given to her, and are united with her as part of her visible bodily structure and through her with Christ, who rules her through the Supreme Pontiff and the bishops. The bonds which bind men to the Church in a visible way are profession of faith, the sacraments, and ecclesiastical government and communion. He is not saved, however, who, though part of the body of the Church, does not persevere in charity. He remains indeed in the bosom of the Church, but, as it were, only in a "bodily" manner and not "in his heart" (cf. S. Augustinus, *Bapt. c. Donat.* V, 28, 39: PL 43, 19). "Surely it is obvious that what is said, inside the Church and outside, is to be understood according to the heart, and not according to the body" (cf. *ib.,* III, 19, 26: col. 152; V, 18, 24: col. 189, *In Io.* Tr. 61, 2: PL 35, 1800). All the Church's children should remember that their exalted status is to be attributed not to their own merits but to the special grace of Christ. If they fail moreover to respond to that grace in thought, word and deed, not only shall they not be saved but they will be the more severely judged (cf. Luke 12:48: "Of everyone to whom much has been given, much will be required" (cf. also Matt. 5:19-20; 7:21-22; 25:41-46; Jas. 2:14).

Catechumens who, moved by the Holy Spirit, seek with explicit intention to be incorporated into the Church are by that very intention joined with her. With love and solicitude Mohter Church already embraces them as her own.

DOGMATIC CONSTITUTION ON THE CHURCH, n. 14

The Church is believed to be indefectibly holy. Indeed Christ, the Son of God, who with the Father and the Spirit is praised as "uniquely holy" (Missale Romanum, *Gloria in excelsis;* cf. Luke 1:35; Mark 1:24; Luke 4:34; John 6:69; Acts 3:14; 4:27 et 30; Heb. 7:26; 1 John 2:20; Apoc. 3:7), loved the Church as His bride, delivered Himself up for her. He did this that He might sanctify her (cf. Eph. 5:25-26). He united her to Himself as His own body and brought it to perfection by the gift of the Holy Spirit for God's glory. Therefore in the Church, everyone whether belonging to the hierarchy, or being cared for by it, is called to holiness, according to the saying of the Apostle: "For this is the will of God, your sanctification" (1 Thess. 4:3; Eph. 1:4). However, this holiness of the Church is unceasingly manifested, and must be manifested, in the fruits of grace which the Spirit produces in the faithful; it is expressed in many ways in individuals, who in their walk of life, tend toward the perfection of charity, thus causing the edification of others; in a very special way this (holiness) appears in the practice of the counsels, customarily called "evangelical." This practice of the counsels, under the implusion of the Holy Spirit, undertaken by many Christians, either privately or in a Church-approved condition or state of life, gives and must give in the world an outstanding witness and example of this same holiness.

DOGMATIC CONSTITUTION ON THE CHURCH, n. 39

The Church was founded for the purpose of spreading the kingdom of Christ throughout the earth for the glory of God the Father, to enable all men to share in His saving redemption (cf. Pius XI, encyclical *Rerum Ecclesiae*: AAS 18 [1926] p. 65), and that through them the whole world might enter into a relationship with Christ. All activity of the Mystical Body directed to the attainment of this goal is called the apostolate, which the Church carries on in various ways through all her members. For the Christian vocation by its very nature is also a vocation to the apostolate. No part of the structure of a living body is merely passive but has a share in the functions as well as life of the body: so, too, in the body of Christ, which is the Church, "the whole body . . . in keeping with the proper activity of each part, derives its increase from its own internal development" (Eph. 4:16).

Indeed, the organic union in this body and the structure of the members are so compact that the member who fails to make his proper contribution to the development of the Church must be said to be useful neither to the Church nor to himself.

DECREE ON THE APOSTOLATE OF THE LAITY, n. 2

Each individual part contributes through its special gifts to the good of the other parts and of the whole Church. Through the common sharing of gifts and through the common effort to attain fullness in unity, the whole and each of the parts receive increase. Not only, then, is the people of God made up of different peoples but in its inner structure also it is composed of various ranks. This diversity among its members arises either by reason of their duties, as is the case with those who exercise the sacred ministry for the good of their brethren, or by reason of their condition and state of life, as is the case with those many who enter the religious state and, tending toward holiness by a narrower path, stimulate their brethren by their example. Moreover, within the Church particular Churches hold a rightful place; these Churches retain their own traditions, without in any way opposing the primacy of the Chair of Peter, which presides over the whole assembly of charity (cf. S. Ignatius M., *Ad Rom.*, Praef.: Ed. Funk, I, p.

252), and protects legitimate differences, while at the same time assuring that such differences do not hinder unity but rather contribute toward it. Between all the parts of the Church there remains a bond of close communion whereby they share spiritual riches, apostolic workers and temporal resources. For the members of the people of God are called to share these goods in common, and of each of the Churches the words of the Apostle hold good: "According to the gift that each has received, administer it to one another as good stewards of the manifold grace of God" (1 Pet. 4:10).

DOGMATIC CONSTITUTION ON THE CHURCH, n. 13

In the Church there is a diversity of ministry but a oneness of mission. Christ conferred on the Apostles and their successors the duty of teaching, sanctifying, and ruling in His name and power. But the laity likewise share in the priestly, prophetic, and royal office of Christ and therefore have their own share in the mission of the whole people of God in the Church and in the world.

They exercise the apostolate in fact by their activity directed to the evangelization and sanctification of men and to the penetrating and perfecting of the temporal order through the spirit of the Gospel. In this way, their temporal activity openly bears witness to Christ and promotes the salvation of men. Since the laity, in accordance with their state of life, live in the midst of the world and its concerns, they are called by God to exercise their apostolate in the world like leaven, with the ardor of the spirit of Christ.

DECREE ON THE APOSTOLATE OF THE LAITY, n. 2

The Church has not been really founded, and is not yet fully alive, nor is it a perfect sign of Christ among men, unless there is a laity worthy of the name working along with the hierarchy. For the Gospel cannot be deeply grounded in the abilities, life and work of any people without the active presence of laymen. Therefore, even at the very founding of a Church, great attention is to be paid to establishing a mature, Christian laity.

DECREE ON THE MISSIONARY ACTIVITY OF THE CHURCH, n. 21

As God loved us with an unselfish love, so also the faithful should in their charity care for the human person himself, loving him with the same affection with which God sought out man. Just as Christ, then, went about all the towns and villages, curing every kind of disease and infirmity as a sign that the kingdom of God had come (cf. Matt. 9:35 ff; Acts 10:38), so also the Church, through her children, is one with men of every condition, but especially with the poor and the afflicted. For them, she gladly spends and is spent (cf. 2 Cor. 12:15), sharing in their joys and sorrows, knowing of their longings and problems, suffering with them in death's anxieties. To those in quest of peace, she wishes to answer in fraternal dialogue, bearing them the peace and the light of the Gospel.

Let Christians labor and collaborate with others in rightly regulating the affairs of social and economic life. With special care, let them devote themselves to the education of children and young people by means of different kinds of schools, which should be considered not only as the most excellent means of forming and developing Christian youth, but also as a valuable public service, especially in the developing nations, working toward the uplifting of human dignity, and toward better living conditions. Furthermore, let them take part in the strivings of those people who, waging war on famine, ignorance, and disease, are struggling to better their way of life and to secure peace in the world. In this activity, the faithful should be eager to offer prudent aid to projects sponsored by public and private organizations, by governments, by various Christian communities, and even by non-Christian religions.

DECREE ON THE MISSION ACTIVITY OF THE CHURCH, n. 12

The intimate partnership of married life and love has been established by the Creator and qualified by His laws, and is rooted in the conjugal covenant of irrevocable personal consent. Hence by that human act whereby spouses mutually bestow and accept each other a relationship arises which by divine will and in the eyes of society too is a lasting one. For the good of the spouses and their off-springs as well as of society, the existence of the sacred bond no longer depends on human decisions alone. For, God Himself is the author of matrimony, endowed as it is with various benefits and purposes (cf. St. Augustine, *De Bene coniugali* PL 40, 375-376 and 394; St. Thomas, *Summa Theologica*, Suppl. Quaest. 49, art 3 ad 1). All of these have a very decisive bearing on the continuation of the human race, on the personal development and eternal destiny of the individual members of a family, and on the dignity, stability, peace and prosperity of the family itself and of human society as a whole. By their very nature, the institution of matrimony itself and conjugal love are ordained for the procreation and education of children, and find in them their ultimate crown. Thus a man and a woman, who by their compact of conjugal love "are no longer two, but one flesh" (Matt. 19:6), render mutual help and service to each other through an intimate union of their persons and of their actions. Through this union they experience the meaning of their oneness and attain to it with growing perfection day by day. As a mutual gift of two persons, this intimate union and the good of the children impose total fidelity on the spouses and argue for an unbreakable oneness between them (cf. Pius XI, Encyclical Letter *Casti Connubii* AAS 22 [1930], pp. 546-547; Denz.-Schoen. 3706).

Christ the Lord abundantly blessed this many-faceted love, welling up as it does from the fountain of divine love and structured as it is on the model of His union with His Church. For as God of old made Himself present (cf. Osee 2; Jer. 3:6-13; Ezech. 16, 23; Is. 54) to His people through a covenant of love and fidelity, so now the Savior of men and the Spouse (cf. Matt. 9:15; Mark 2:19-20; Luke 5:34-35; John 3:29; cf. also 2 Cor. 11:2; Eph. 5:27; Apoc. 19:7-8; 2, 9) of the Church comes into the lives of married Christians through the sacrament of matrimony. He abides with them thereafter so that just as He loved the Church and handed Himself over on her behalf (cf. Eph. 5:25), the spouses may love each other with perpetual fidelity through mutual self-bestowal.

PASTORAL CONSTITUTION ON THE CHURCH IN THE MODERN WORLD, n. 48

In order to continue doing the will of His Father in the world, Christ works unceasingly through the Church. He operates through His ministers, and hence He remains always the source and wellspring of the unity of their lives. Priests, then, can achieve this coordination and unity of life by joining themselves with Christ to acknowledge the will of the Father. For them this means a complete gift of themselves to the flock committed to them (cf. 1 John 3:16). Hence, as they fulfill the role of the Good Shepherd, in the very exercise of their pastoral charity they will discover a bond of priestly perfection which draws their life and activity to unity and coordination. This pastoral charity ("May it be a duty of love to feed the Lord's flock" [St. Augustine, "tract on John," 123, 5: PL 35, 1967]), flows out in a very special way from the Eucharistic Sacrifice. This stands as the root and center of the whole life of a priest. What takes place on the altar of sacrifice, the priestly heart must make his own. This cannot be done unless priests through prayer continue to penetrate more deeply into the mystery of Christ.

DECREE ON THE MINISTRY AND LIFE OF PRIESTS, n. 14

The Church of Christ is truly present in all legitimate local congregations of the faithful which, united with their pastors, are themselves called churches in the New Testament (cf. Acts 8:1; 14: 22-23; 20:17). For in their locality these are the new People called by God, in the Holy Spirit and in much fullness. In them the faithful are gathered together by preaching of the Gospel of Christ, and the mystery of the Lord's Supper is celebrated, that by the food and blood of the Lord's body the whole brotherhood may be joined together. In any community of the altar, under the sacred ministry of the bishop (cf. S. Ignatius M., Smyrn. 8, 1: ed. Funk, I, p. 282), there is exhibited a symbol of that charity and "unity of the mystical Body, without which there can be no salvation" (S. Thomas, *Summa Theol.* III. q. 73, a. 3). In these communities, though frequently small and poor, or living in the Diaspora, Christ is present, and in virtue of His presence there is brought together one, holy, catholic and apostolic Church (cf. S. Augustinus, C. *Faustum*, 12, 20: PL 42, 265; *Serm.* 57, 7: PL 38, 389, etc.). For "the partaking of the body and blood of Christ does nothing other than make us be transformed into that which we consume."

DOGMATIC CONSTITUTION ON
THE CHURCH, n. 26

As the Son was sent by the Father (cf. Jn. 20:21), so He too sent the Apostles, saying: "Go, therefore, make disciples of all nations, baptizing them in the name of the Father and of the Son and of the Holy Spirit, teaching them to observe all things whatsoever I have commanded you. And behold I am with you all days even to the consummation of the world" (Mt. 21:18-20). The Church has received this solemn mandate of Christ to proclaim the saving truth from the apostles and must carry it out to the very ends of the earth (cf. Acts 1:8). Wherefore she makes the words of the Apostle her own: "Woe to me, if I do not preach the Gospel" (1 Cor. 9:16), and continues unceasingly to send heralds of the Gospel until such time as the infant churches are fully established and can themselves continue the work of evangelizing. For the Church is compelled by the Holy Spirit to do her part that God's plan may be fully realized, whereby He has constituted Christ as the source of salvation for the whole world. By the proclamation of the Gospel she prepares her hearers to receive and profess the faith. She gives them the dispositions necessary for baptism, snatches them from the slavery of error and of idols and incorporates them in Christ so that through charity they may grow up into full maturity in Christ. Through her work, whatever good is in the minds and hearts of men, whatever good lies latent in the religious practices and cultures of diverse peoles, is not only saved from destruction but is also cleansed, raised up and perfected unto the glory of God, the confusion of the devil and the happiness of man. The obligation of spreading the faith is imposed on every disciple of Christ according to his state (cf. Benedictus XV, Epist. Apost. *Maximum illud*: AAS 11 (1919) p. 440, especially 451 ff. Pius XI, Litt. Encycl. *Rerum Ecclesiae*: AAS 18 (1926) pp. 68-69. Pius XII, Litt. Encycl. *Fidei Donum*, 21 apr. 1957: AAS 49 (1957) pp. 236-237). Although, however, all the faithful can baptize, the priest alone can complete the building up of the Body in the eucharistic sacrifice. Thus are fulfilled the words of God, spoken through His prophet: "From the rising of the sun until the going down thereof my name is great among the gentiles, and in every place a clean oblation is sacrificed and offered up in my name" (Mal. 1:11; cf. *Didaché*, 14: ed. Funk, I, p. 32. S. Iustinus, *Dial.* 41: PG 6, 564. S. Irenaeus, *Adv. Haer.* IV, 17, 5; PG 7, 1023; Harvey, 2, p. 199 s. Conc. Trid., Sess. 22, cap. 1; Denz. 939

[1742]). In this way the Church both prays and labors in order that the entire world may become the People of God, the Body of the Lord and the Temple of the Holy Spirit, and that in Christ, the Head of all, all honor and glory may be rendered to the Creator and Father of the Universe. DOGMATIC CONSTITUTION ON THE CHURCH, n. 17

The Church, sent to all peoples of every time and place, is not bound exclusively and indissolubly to any race or nation, any particular way of life or any customary way of life recent or ancient. Faithful to her own tradition and at the same time conscious of her universal mission, she can enter into communion with the various civilizations, to their enrichment and the enrichment of the Church herself.

PASTORAL CONSTITUTION ON THE CHURCH IN THE MODERN WORLD, n. 58

Inspired by no earthly ambition, the Church seeks but a solitary goal: to carry forward the work of Christ under the lead of the befriending Spirit. And Christ entered this world to give witness to the truth, to rescue and not to sit in judgment, to serve and not to be served (cf. John 18:37; Matt. 20:28; Mark 10:45). PASTORAL CONSTITUTION ON CHURCH IN THE MODERN WORLD, n. 3

Missionary activity is closely bound up even with human nature itself and its aspirations. For by manifesting Christ the Church reveals to men the real truth about their condition and their whole calling, since Christ is the source and model of that redeemed humanity, imbued with brotherly love, sincerity and a peaceful spirit, to which they all aspire. Christ and the Church, which bears witness to Him by preaching the Gospel, transcend every peculiarity of race or nation and therefore cannot be considered foreign anywhere or to anybody. Christ Himself is the way and the truth, which the preaching of the Gospel opens to all in proclaiming in the hearing of all these words of Christ: "Repent, and believe the Gospel" (Mark 1:15). Now, since he who does not believe is already judged (cf. John 3:18), the words of Christ are at one and the same time words of judgment and of grace, of death and of life. For it is only by putting to death what is old that we are able to approach the newness of life. This is true first of all about persons, but it holds also for the various goods of this world which bear the mark both of man's sin and of God's blessing: "For all have sinned and have need of the glory of God" (Rom. 3:23). No one is freed from sin by himself and by his own power, no one is raised above himself, no one is completely rid of his sickness or his solitude or his servitude (cf. Irenaeus, *Adv. Haer.*, III, 15, n. 3 (PG 7, 919): "Veritatis . . ." "They were preachers of truth and apostles of liberty"). On the contrary, all stand in need of Christ, their model, their mentor, their liberator, their Savior, their source of life. The Gospel has truly been a leaven of liberty and progress in human history, even in the temporal sphere, and always proves itself a leaven of brotherhood, of unity and of peace. Not without cause is Christ hailed by the faithful as "the expected of the nations, and their Savior."

DECREE ON THE MISSION ACTIVITY OF THE CHURCH, n. 8

Divinely sent to the nations of the world to be unto them "a universal sacrament of salvation," the Church, driven by the inner necessity of her own catholicity, and obeying the mandate of her Founder (cf. Mark 16:16), strives ever to proclaim the Gospel to all men. The Apostles themselves, on whom the Church was founded, following in the footsteps of Christ, "preached the word of truth and begot churches." It is the duty of their successors to make this task endure "so that the word of God may run and be glorified" (2 Thess. 3:1) and the kingdom of God be proclaimed and established throughout the world.

In the present state of affairs, out of which there is arising a new situation for mankind, the Church, being the salt of the earth and the light of the world (cf. Matt. 5:13-14), is more urgently called upon to save and renew every creature, that all things may be restored in Christ and all men may constitute one family in Him and one people of God.

DECREE ON THE MISSION ACIVITY
OF THE CHURCH, n. 1

The remedy which must be applied to atheism is to be sought in a proper presentation of the Church's teaching as well as in the integral life of the Church and her members. For it is the function of the Church, led by the Holy Spirit Who renews and purifies her ceaselessly, to make God the Father and His Incarnate Son present and in a sense visible. This result is achieved chiefly by the witness of a living and mature faith, namely, one trained to see difficulties clearly and to master them. Many martyrs have given luminous witness to this faith and continue to do so. This faith needs to prove its fruitfulness by penetrating the believer's entire life, including its worldly dimensions, and by activating him toward justice and love, especially regarding the needy. What does the most reveal God's presence, however, is the brotherly charity of the faithful who are united in spirit as they work together for the faith of the Gospel (cf. Phil. 1:27) and who prove themselves a sign of unity.

PASTORAL CONSTITUTION ON THE CHURCH IN THE MODERN WORLD, n. 21

In order to be faithful to the divine command, "teach all nations" (Matt. 28:19-20), the Catholic Church must work with all urgency and concern "that the word of God be spread abroad and glorified (2 Thess. 3:1). Hence the Church earnestly begs of its children that, "first of all, supplications, prayers, petitions, acts of thanksgiving be made for all men. . . . For this is good and agreeable in the sight of God our Savior, who wills that all men be saved and come to the knowledge of the truth" (1 Tim. 2.1-4). In the formation of their consciences, the Christian faithful ought to attend to the sacred and certain doctrine of the Church (cf. Pius XII, Radio Message, March 23, 1952: AAS 44 (1952), pp. 270-278). For the Church is, by the will of Christ, the teacher of the truth. It is her duty to give utterance to, and authoritatively to teach, that truth which is Christ Himself, and also to declare and confirm by her authority those principles of the moral order which have their origins in human nature itself. Furthermore, let Christians walk in wisdom in the face of those outside, "in the Holy Spirit, in unaffected love, in the word of truth" (2 Cor. 6:6-7), and let them be about their task of spreading the light of life with all confidence (cf. Acts 4:29) and apostolic courage, even to the shedding of their blood.

The disciple is bound by a grave obligation toward Christ, his Master, ever more fully to understand the truth received from Him, faithfully to proclaim it, and vigorously to defend it, never—be it understood—having recourse to means that are incompatible with the spirit of the Gospel. At the same time, the charity of Christ urges him to love and have prudence and patience in his dealings with those who are in error or in ignorance with regard to the faith (cf. John XXIII, Encyclical Letter, *Pacem in Terris*, April 11, 1963: AAS 55 (1963), pp. 299-300). All is to be taken into account—the Christian duty to Christ, the life-giving word which must be proclaimed, the rights of the human person, and the measure of grace granted by God through Christ to men who are invited freely to accept and profess the faith.

DECLARATION ON RELIGIOUS FREEDOM, n. 14

Christ's redemptive work, while essentially concerned with the salvation of men, includes also the renewal of the whole temporal order. Hence the mission of the Church is not only to bring the message and grace of Christ to men but also to penetrate and perfect the temporal order with the spirit of the Gospel. In fulfilling this mission of the Church, the Christian laity exercise their apostolate both in the Church and in the world, in both the spiritual and temporal orders. These orders, although distinct, are so connected in the singular plan of God that He Himself intends to raise up the whole world again in Christ and make it a new creation, initially on earth and completely on the last day. In both orders the layman, being simultaneously a believer and a citizen, should be continuously led by the same Christian conscience.

DECREE ON THE APOSTOLATE OF THE LATIY, n. 5

The Gospel of Christ constantly renews the life and culture of fallen man; it combats and removes the errors and evils resulting from the permanent allurement of sin. It never ceases to purify and elevate the morality of peoples. By riches coming from above, it makes fruitful, as it were from within, the spiritual qualities and traditions of every people and of every age. It strengthens, perfects and restores them in Christ (cf. Eph. 1:10). Thus the Church, in the very fulfillment of her own function stimulates and advances human and civic culture; by her action, also by her liturgy, she leads men toward interior liberty.

PASTORAL CONSTITUTION ON THE CHURCH IN THE MODERN WORLD, n. 58

In a special way, the duty of educating belongs to the Church, not merely because she must be recognized as a human society capable of educating, but especially because she has the responsibility of announcing the way of salvation to all men, of communicating the life of Christ to those who believe, and, in her unfailing solicitude, of assisting men to be able to come to the fullness of this life (cf. Pius XI's encyclical letter, *Divini Illius Magistri*, 1, pp. 53 ff.

and 56 ff.). The Church is bound as a mother to give to these children of hers an education by which their whole life can be imbued with the spirit of Christ and at the same time do all she can to promote for all peoples the complete perfection of the human person, the good of earthly society and the building of a world that is more human.

DECLARATION ON CHRISTIAN EDUCATION, n. 3

Just as it is in the world's interest to acknowledge the Church as an historical reality, and to recognize her good influence, so the Church herself knows how richly she has profited by the history and development of humanity.

The experience of past ages, the progress of the sciences, and the treasures hidden in the various forms of human culture, by all of which the nature of man himself is more clearly revealed and new roads to truth are opened, these profit the Church, too. For, from the beginning of her history she has learned to express the message of Christ with the help of the ideas and terminology of various philosophers, and has tried to clarify it with their wisdom, too. Her purpose has been to adapt the Gospel to the grasp of all as well as to the needs of the learned, insofar as such was appropriate. Indeed this accommodated preaching of the revealed word ought to remain the law of all evangelization. For thus the ability to express Christ's message in its own way is developed in each nation, and at the same time there is fostered a living exchange between the Church and the diverse cultures of people. To promote such exchange, especially in our days, the Church requires the special help of those who live in the world, are versed in different institutions and specialties, and grasp their innermost significance in the eyes of both believers and unbelievers. With the help of the Holy Spirit, it is the task of the entire People of God, especially pastors and theologians, to hear, distinguish and interpret the many voices of our age, and to judge them in the light of the divine word, so that revealed truth can always be more deeply penetrated, better understood and set forth to greater advantage.

PASTORAL CONSTITUTION ON THE CHURCH IN THE MODERN WORLD, n. 44

Since the Church has a visible and social structure as a sign of her unity in Christ, she can and ought to be enriched by the development of human social life, not that there is any lack in the constitution given her by Christ, but that she can understand it more penetratingly, express it better, and adjust it more successfully to our times. Moreover, she gratefully understands that in her community life no less than in her individual sons, she receives a variety of helps from men of every rank and condition, for whoever promotes the human community at the family level, culturally, in its economic, social and political dimensions, both nationally and internationally, such a one, according to God's design, is contributing greatly to the Church as well, to the extent that she depends on things outside herself. Indeed, the Church admits that she has greatly profited and still profits from the antagonism of those who oppose or who persecute her.

PASTORAL CONSTITUTION ON THE CHURCH IN THE MODERN WORLD, n. 44

That the earthly and the heavenly city penetrate each other is a fact accessible to faith alone; it remains a mystery of human history, which sin will keep in great disarray until the splendor of God's sons is fully revealed. Pursuing the saving purpose which is proper to her, the Church does not only communicate divine life to men but in some way casts the reflected light of that life over the entire earth, most of all by its healing and elevating impact on the dignity of the person, by the way in which it strengthens the seams of human society and imbues the everyday activity of men with a deeper meaning and importance. Thus through her individual members and her whole community, the Church believes she can contribute greatly toward making the family of man and its history more human.

PASTORAL CONSTITUTION ON THE CHURCH IN THE MODERN WORLD, n. 40